LIFE INSTEAD

LIFE INSTEAD

DIANE BRINGGOLD

Special Edition for
THE CHRISTIAN QUALITY
PAPERBACK BOOK CLUB

WORD BOOKS
PUBLISHER
WACO, TEXAS

ISBN 0–8499–3910–0
Library of Congress catalog card number: 79–63931
Printed in the United States of America

Scripture quotations are from The Revised Standard Version of the Bible, copyright 1946, 1952, © 1971, 1973 by the Division of Christian Education of the National Council of the Churches of Christ in the U.S.A., and are used by permission.

To
the Holy Spirit,
the true Author of this book

CONTENTS

- 1 -

THE END

Oh my God, Bruce, the trees!"

I screamed. Bruce, at the controls, saw them too. Instantly, he reacted, banking the plane sharply left, but not in time to avoid the onrushing mountainside.

I remember the crash landing did not seem as rough as I expected. Then . . . it was all over . . . the end . . . the end of everything . . . nothing . . .

I don't know how long I was unconscious, but probably no more than a few moments. Suddenly I was aware of the flames bursting out from below the instrument panel. I still had my seatbelt on, but I had slid down in my seat. Bruce was leaning on top of me. He wasn't moving. There was no sound at all in the plane except the crackling of the flames. They were searing my legs, my hands, my face. Instinctively I had thrown my hands over my eyes. Somehow, wriggling and squirming, I got my seatbelt unfastened and pushed Bruce off me. He still did not move.

9

I slid out the open door and crawled away from the plane seconds before the gas tank exploded.

* * *

It happened on Monday, December 1, 1975—a date I will never forget. Bruce and I and our three children were flying home after spending a weekend with our friends Bill and Edie LeFevre at their vacation home in Dunsmuir, California, near Mount Shasta. Jim and Virginia Dixon were traveling with us. Our plane was in the shop for repairs, so we had rented another Cessna 210, identical to ours even down to its red and white paint job. Bruce was an experienced pilot, skilled in instrument flying. I too had my pilot's license, but I was a "baby" pilot with less than 100 hours as pilot in command.

We had originally intended to fly home on Sunday. Saturday had brought snow, to the great delight of eleven-year-old Scott, eight-year-old Mary, and five-year-old Laura. Intermittent flurries continued on Sunday, forcing us to wait for more favorable conditions. Monday morning did not bring them, though the snow had stopped.

Soon after breakfast, Bill and Edie, traveling by motor home, left for Ventura. For Jim and Virginia, Bruce and me, the coffeepot did double, triple duty as the hours wore on.

Early in the afternoon, when Bruce called the flight service station for the area, he was informed that the weather was improving to the north. Always cautious, Bruce piled us into the car to drive from Dunsmuir to Shasta so we could check out for ourselves whether conditions were good enough for safe flight. We found a moderately low overcast, but visibility was good below the clouds.

"It seems to be clearing," was Bruce's judgment. "We'll fly north through the valley just past Mount Shasta. Then where the valley widens out, we'll be able to climb through the clouds on instruments until we break into the clear and can turn south to Ventura."

Takeoff from Mott Field in Dunsmuir was uneventful. We headed north below the clouds, keeping our eyes on Highway 5 snaking through the valley below us. Knowing that we would be safe as long as we kept to the left of the highway, we almost began to relax.

The respite was brief. The clouds began to break up, merging into an ominous opaque gray blanket. Looking out the side of the plane, I could no longer see the ground. Fog swirled around us.

Bruce, worry lines etching his forehead, was very quiet, concentrating on flying the plane. The children had lapsed into unaccustomed silence, sensing our tension.

"Bruce, we've got to turn around," I said. I had scarcely gotten all the words out before I realized that would be more dangerous in the confines of the narrow valley than to go on ahead. It was just then I saw the trees and knew we were going to crash.

With the children screaming, "Mommy, mommy!" and Bruce maneuvering to avoid the inevitable, we slammed into Black Butte.

* * *

After the explosion, lying in excruciating pain on the jagged shale of the steep cindercone, I could hear Jim and Virginia calling me. I was thankful they had survived the crash. But I did not answer them. I hid behind a pile of rocks. I wanted to die. I knew my husband and children were dead. I was severely burned. It was the end of my life as a wife and mother . . . the end of my life as a woman who thought she was totally self-sufficient. How could I go on living? ·

- 2 -

THE WAY IT WAS

I was born and raised in Long Beach, California. Our family went to church from time to time, but not on a regular basis. Religion was not an important part of my life as I was growing up. Bruce and I met at Stanford University when I was a senior and he was a first year law student. He had been raised in the Episcopal church, and church had been an important part of his life. When we decided to get married, I began to attend an adult confirmation class at All Saints' Episcopal Church in Long Beach. I chose that particular church because I thought it would be the prettiest Episcopal church to be married in. During the year Bruce and I were engaged I was living at home and working in Los Angeles as a parole agent trainee for the California Youth Authority.

The priest at All Saints', the Reverend James E. Carroll, was truly a man of God, a committed Christian. Under his guidance, I came to know Jesus as my Lord and Savior. On the Day of Pentecost in 1961 I formally accepted Jesus as my Savior and was baptized and confirmed.

Bruce and I were married in July and returned to Stanford. My training period completed, I was able to work as a parole agent out of the Youth Authority's San Francisco office. Bruce completed his final year of law school and was hired by the district attorney's office in Ventura. He was to work there for two years before going into private practice with Jim Loebl. At the time of the accident the firm had expanded to include Bill Peck, also a partner, and two attorneys who were employed by the firm.

Upon arriving in Ventura, we became active members of St. Paul's Episcopal Church. As the years passed I was elected to positions of leadership. I was president of two of the women's guilds. I was president of the Episcopal Churchwomen of St. Paul's, and finally I was elected to serve on the vestry, the second woman to do so at St. Paul's. When we established a parish day school, I served on the Board of Education for the school and as co-chairman of the Parent Faculty Fellowship. I was also active in Church Women United and in many community activities. I was trying to live a Christian life, but it is obvious to me now I was trying to do it all myself, without asking the Lord's help or guidance. I had grown up feeling I should be self-reliant, that I should ask for help only as a last resort. Asking for help, even from the Lord, was almost an admission of weakness, of failure in my eyes.

Bruce and I had a wonderful marriage. The first two years we lived in Ventura I continued working for the Youth Authority as an institutional parole agent at the nearby Ventura School for Girls. In 1964, our first child, Scott, was born on October 20. He was supposed

to arrive on my birthday, October 3, but apparently he
didn't like the idea of sharing birthdays. Mary was born
three years later on August 22, 1967, and Laura, the
youngest, was born May 7, 1970. They were bright,
beautiful children.

Scott looked just like his father. They loved to hunt
and fish together, and spent many hours in our yard
playing football and baseball. As with many eleven-year-
old boys, the love of Scott's life was sports. He played
Little League baseball, basketball, and flag football
according to the season. Scott and two friends even
formed a club which they named the "Winner's Club,"
just to earn money to buy tickets to professional sports
events, especially Los Angeles Dodgers baseball games.
The boys did chores around the neighborhood, col-
lected newspapers and aluminum cans, and made and
sold Christmas decorations. The girls were auxiliary
members of the club, and all of them had matching club
shirts and baseball caps.

Mary, a beautiful blond, was the worrier of the family.
She took life very seriously. Not to be outdone by her
brother, she too had a club, a cooking club. Each week
five of her friends would come to our home to learn to
cook something. If I was busy, they might make root
beer floats, but we also made fancier things like castle
cakes. If the club met on a school holiday, they would
sometimes fix lunch for the Winner's Club. Not bad for
third-graders. My kitchen was often a mess, but helping
the girls learn to cook was fun for me too.

Laura, our brunette, was the most affectionate member of the family. Like many youngest children, she was
slightly spoiled and could twist both Scott and Mary
around her finger. In kindergarten she had not yet
formed a club of her own, but she often invited her

friends over to play and tagged along after Scott and Mary, joining in their activities.

All three children enjoyed each other's company. In fact, I feel really fortunate that they not only loved each other, they also liked each other. They had shared a room together until three months before the accident, when we added a third bedroom and a family room to our home.

I was also blessed in my marriage. When we arrived in Ventura, Bruce and I owned our wedding gifts, two typewriters, a small television set, and a 1959 Volkswagen. We owed money to both Princeton University, where Bruce had earned his Bachelor of Arts Degree, and to Stanford. Bruce was anxious to establish a successful law practice but, unlike many men who are busy establishing a successful business or career, Bruce never felt his law practice was as important as his family. He worked hard and loved the practice of law. He was active in many community organizations, but he always set aside time to be with his family.

We traveled widely in our plane and had many wonderful vacations together. Some were family vacations and some were just for the two of us—times to get to know one another better and to keep our love alive and growing. How lucky I am we had those times together. Many couples and families live a whole lifetime together and never share the experiences we shared.

In common with all women, wives, and mothers, I had problems—at least I thought I did. You know, when am I going to find time for myself, how am I ever going to get everything done today—things like that. Ordinary everyday problems. Nothing I couldn't handle. I was self-sufficient, I thought.

- 3 -

THE BEGINNING

Diane, Diane, where are you?" I could still hear Jim
and Virginia calling me.

Hiding among the jagged rocks, I remained silent. If
they think I am dead, I reasoned, maybe the rescuers
won't look too hard for me.

I wondered how long it would take me to die if they
didn't find me.

I was lying with my back to the wreckage of the plane,
which was still burning. I couldn't look at it. Bruce,
Scott, Mary, Laura . . . they were all in that plane. I
think they were dead before the fire started, but I really
don't know. I do know that as I huddled down among
the rocks, the thought kept running through my mind
that my life was over. All my plans for the future had
died with my family.

As the minutes elapsed, the sensation of emptiness
gave way to intense pain. I was aware my face and hands
were badly burned, charred when the instrument panel
had burst into flames and forced me out of the plane. I
can't face the pain, I thought. I have no tolerance for

17

pain. Even the sight of a needle terrifies me, but burns were the injury I had always feared most. I placed the back of my hands on a snow-covered rock to ease the pain. I wished it were colder so I could freeze to death quickly.

Suddenly something caused me to look up. About eight or ten feet away, I saw a white-robed figure. The figure was radiant, but the radiance did not dispel the fog. It seemed to be a man, though I couldn't distinguish his features clearly. Somehow I knew it was the Lord.

"Diane." His voice was warm but full of authority. "It is not up to you to decide whether to live or die. That decision is mine alone to make."

I don't know why, but somehow I was not surprised that he was there with me, that he was speaking to me. I wanted him to know that I really couldn't go on living. "Lord, that's easy for you to say, but I can't face being widowed, being childless, and being badly burned. Two out of three maybe, but not all three." I wasn't trying to bargain with him. I did not expect him to restore my husband or my children or to heal me, although he could have. I just wanted him to know it was the combination of circumstances that had overwhelmed me.

He remained silent, as if he were waiting for me to continue. "Lord," I said, "if you want me to live, I will give *you* my life. I will give *you* my problems. You will have to cope with the pain, with the loneliness, and with the grief. I can't." Still he did not speak, but such love flowed from him that I knew he would care for me—that he would handle the grief, the pain, the loneliness. I knew that I was in his care and that everything would be all right.

He had given me a precious gift—the gift of faith. Since that afternoon I have never doubted he is with me. I know I can trust him completely. Psalm 34:17 says, "When a man cries for help, the Lord hears him and sets him free from all his troubles" (NEB). He truly does.

As suddenly as he had appeared, The Lord was no longer there. I don't know how long he had been with me there on the mountain—a few minutes or a few seconds. Time was unimportant.

Faintly in the distance I heard cars passing on Highway 5 at the foot of Black Butte. I heard Jim and Virginia crying for help. They were no longer calling my name. I called to them, "Jim, Virginia, I'm okay. I'm up above you."

I came out of my hiding place, scooting gingerly on my seat across the sharp rocks. With my injuries and the steep terrain, I hadn't progressed very far when the first of the rescuers arrived. His name was Jim Cain. He had heard the crash while out working in his corral. He helped me further down the hill. I asked him not to take me too close to the Dixons. I did not want them to see how badly I was injured. I knew my face was a mess.

When he had made sure we were all safe, he left to go up to the plane. I told him not to. I told him everyone else was dead. I was sobbing uncontrollably.

While Mr. Cain was investigating the plane to see if anyone else had survived, three young people arrived. I believe their names were Ann, Danny, and John, and they seemed to be college age. The boys put their jackets on the ground for me to lie on, then left to see if they could help Jim and Virginia. Ann stayed with me, holding me in her arms until the rescue team arrived. I remember saying to her, "You're really brave to hold me, looking like I do." Squeamish as I am, comforting someone whose face was a charred, bloody mess would have been beyond my capabilities. But she said, "No, you're the brave one." We passed the time arguing about who was the bravest. I also remember telling her my name and the names of my husband and children, and someone—I'm not sure who—who to notify of the accident. I gave them my mother's name and the names of Bruce's parents and also his partners Jim Loebl and Bill Peck. I remember stressing that Jim or Bill should be notified first so they could break the news to Bruce's parents. I did not want Howard and Irene to be told over the phone. I think everyone thought I was in shock and did not know what I was saying. Fortunately, when the sheriff in Ojai was notified, he did call Jim Loebl first.

I was still in excruciating pain. I rejoiced when a man came over to me and introduced himself as Dr. Knudson. He had climbed Black Butte in the dark to render his aid. In his medical kit he had one shot of morphine. I don't know if I was in any more pain than Jim and Virginia, but my injuries were the most obvious and I got the morphine. Usually I am really leery of drugs, but that night I didn't care if I got hooked if the medication would help the pain. I think that is the only shot in my life I have ever welcomed. It did ease the pain. I know Dr. Knudson was being used by God that night to ease my suffering. He may not be aware of it even now.

More and more people began to arrive. The sheriff who was in charge of the rescue that night told me later he had never had so many people arrive on the scene of an accident volunteering to help. I was told Jim, Virginia, and I would be taken down one at a time.

Black Butte is a cindercone, the remnant of a dead volcano. The ground is loose shale and every step anyone takes starts a miniature landslide. If each of us was not off the mountain before the rescuers began lowering the next one, we would be endangered by falling rocks. Virginia was the first to be carried down. I was the second.

I don't remember much about that stretcher ride down the mountain. I think two men carried the stretcher and at least two other men helped them, walking alongside. I know that belaying lines were attached to the stretcher. The lines were secured around a tree or a large rock, whatever was available, then slowly released, so that if the men carrying the stretcher slipped the stretcher with me on it would not go careening down the mountainside. Because of the difficult terrain, the darkness, and the fog, I knew all those men were risking their lives to carry us to safety. I could not believe how carefully they carried the stretcher trying to ease the bumps and jolts as much as possible. I think it took at least three hours to get us all down the mountain and to the waiting ambulance.

We were taken to Eskaton Mt. Shasta Healthcare Center. Outside, filming our arrival there were television crews as well as newspaper photographers. I remember the bright lights when we entered the center. I did not think Jim and Virginia were seriously injured. I was glad for that.* It had been partly at my suggestion the trip had been planned and I remember thinking that if it had not been for my suggestion they would not have been in the plane.

---

*I later learned that they too had suffered extensive second and third degree burns.

The doctors had to cut my wedding ring to remove it from my finger, which was swelling rapidly. They were very careful to cut it only on one side so it could be easily repaired. I thought that was rather silly. I remember saying, "Cut it in half if you need to. I'm not married anymore anyway." The ring was no longer important now that Bruce was dead. I remember the doctors and nurses cutting my clothes so they could be easily removed. I don't remember much else.

It seemed to me we were remaining at Eskaton much longer than necessary. Even after my wounds had been wrapped gently in bandages we remained. I thought I heard them say they were having difficulty getting two ambulances to take us to Chico. Months later Bill Peck told me one reason we remained at Eskaton was that my vital signs were so unstable the doctors were afraid I would not survive the trip down the mountain. I was really amazed. I never considered my condition critical. For some reason the Lord wanted me to live. I knew I would.

Finally we were put in the ambulances. Virginia and I were in one, Jim in the other. What a ride! If you are a backseat driver like me, believe me, riding in the back of an ambulance is a hair-raising experience. I couldn't see out so I never knew when to apply the brakes. I could tell when we passed through a town because it was only then that the siren was turned on. Careening around one sharp curve in the mountain road, Virginia's gurney came loose and slid across the floor. The nurse riding with us secured it again and warned the driver to take the curves more carefully. The rest of the ride was uneventful.

My new life was beginning!

- 4 -

IN MY COCOON

December 2, 1975, 1:30 A.M. My first memory of Chico Community Memorial Hospital is of a sea of faces bending over me. Faces in masks and funny green hats. The doctors and nurses all introduced themselves to me but it would be days and, in some cases, weeks before I got all the names straight. One thing I did know that night. I knew that all those doctors and nurses would be used by the Lord to be channels of his healing.

Dr. L. Richard Morgan told me he was taking me to surgery to remove some of the damaged tissue from my right hand and to make incisions to preserve the deep circulation in the hand. In Dr. Morgan, the doctor on call for the burn unit that night, the Lord provided just the right man at the right time. Dr. Morgan is a plastic surgeon; he is a Christian; he is a physician in the true sense of the word. He knows that to achieve the best medical results you must take into account the needs of the whole person—body, mind, and spirit. When I arrived at the hospital it was important I receive expert medical treatment. It was also important I receive emotional support, that I be treated with tender loving care. No doctor and no nursing staff could have been more supportive than Dr. Morgan and the nurses in the burn unit.

The burn unit at Chico was small. It had only been established six months before the accident, but I sincerely believe I could not have received better care or better medical treatment anywhere.

In this chapter I want to share with you how the Lord protected me from pain and provided for my physical healing. In the next two chapters I will tell you how he helped me to cope with my loneliness and my grief while I was in the hospital.

I really don't remember a lot about the first couple of days I was in the hospital. I must have been very ill when I arrived because at that point I had absolutely no sense of modesty. I didn't care how much of my body was exposed or whether the nurses tending to my needs were male or female just as long as they were doing what needed to be done. I know that a subclavian I.V. was inserted just above my collarbone so that nourishment and medication could be administered intravenously. A catheter was also inserted to take care of my body's wastes. My head, lower legs, and hands were encased in layer upon layer of bandages. My hands were elevated by means of slings attached to poles on either side of my bed.

The first day in the hospital I was not allowed to eat or drink anything. I remember being constantly thirsty. I was allowed to use mouthwash to rinse out my mouth and I must have gone through quarts of it that first day.

I don't remember much pain at first. I know I was

receiving pain medication but I feel the Lord was also protecting me from pain. Swathed in my bandages, I felt as if I was in a lovely soft cocoon. I had suffered a compression fracture in my back. The only time I had any back pain was the day I was taken for x-rays. While I was lying on the cold, hard x-ray table, a problem developed with the x-ray machine. I was left lying on the table while the problem was remedied. *That* day my back *hurt!* Although I do not remember much pain, I do remember being very warm. Most burn patients suffer from the opposite problem, but with my arms elevated, my movement was restricted and my body heat warmed the mattress beneath me until it felt as if I was lying on a heating pad. The bandages on my head, hands, and legs also prevented my body heat from being dissipated.

Lying on your back with your arms in the air is not a natural position. Even though my arms were elevated by means of slings, my shoulder muscles would become stiff and cramp. An enthusiastic young man named O. D. Willhite came by and introduced himself as my physical therapist. The introduction completed, he continued, "I shouldn't say this when you're stuck in here, but it's a beautiful day outside." I replied, "Just because I can't enjoy it doesn't mean I'm not glad it is a lovely day." I meant it. I never wanted my problems to affect those around me. I liked O. D. and I really looked forward to his visits. He would massage my tight neck and shoulder muscles, and it felt great. It is a good thing we got off to a good start. It would not be long before I would dread his visits.

My right hand was so badly burned Dr. Morgan was not sure he would be able to save it. Even if he did succeed in that, he was not sure it would be functional. Time was of the essence if function was to be preserved. On the seventh day after the accident I was taken to surgery where new skin was grafted onto my hand. Before surgery Dr. Morgan had explained that he would take the needed skin from my lower abdomen. After surgery I noticed the bandages were not on my lower abdomen but on my ribcage. It seems Dr. Morgan took one look at the stretch marks on my lower abdomen and decided that skin would never do. I could have told him that, had I realized stretch marks mattered. My kids wanted to leave some evidence I carried them, and it's undeniable.

Until the bandages were removed from my hand there was no way to know whether the grafts would take. During that six-day period all of us were praying. Our prayers were answered! December 14, when the dressings were removed, I was surrounded by handsome men, including Dr. Dale Armstrong, a friend and plastic surgeon from Ventura who was visiting that day. I still remember him and Dr. Morgan discussing my hand as they gently eased off the dressings. They would say *the* hand this, and *the* hand that. Hearing my hand discussed as *the* hand made it sound disembodied. Finally I said, "You know, that hand is still attached to me. So as long as I am awake, could you please refer to it as *her* hand?" They did.

Dr. Morgan and Dr. Armstrong were very pleased with the results of the surgery. They thought my hand really looked good considering the severity of the burns it had suffered. I thought it looked terrible! It was very swollen and very purple. The skin didn't really look like skin; it looked more like cellophane. I remember thinking it would have been perfect to use for one of the monster costumes Scott had liked to wear on Halloween.

As ugly as it was, I thanked God I still had a hand. The grafts had not adhered to the ends of my fingers, however. Eventually new skin would be grafted there. Physical therapy for my hand began almost immediately. It was now I began to dread O. D.'s visits. My hand thought it had suffered enough. It thought it had earned a vacation. After all, the ends of my fingers weren't even covered with skin yet.

We decided my fingers were going to begin to work. At first, even bending them slightly was excruciatingly painful. My little finger complained the most. I remember telling it that it was too small to hurt that much. The end joint had been burned off and there wasn't a lot there to hurt. It seemed to answer back and say just because it was the smallest did not mean it could not scream just as loudly as the other fingers.

I felt sorry for O. D. I knew it was hard for him to inflict the pain that was a necessary part of therapy. I would try not to let him know how much I was hurting until the pain was really too great to bear, and then I would *order* him to stop. I remember apologizing to him one day for being such a sissy. I told him I was sure my pain was nothing compared to what people go through getting large joints to function. He very kindly replied he didn't know any therapy that was more painful than mine. I didn't believe him but it was nice of him to say anyway.

I had mixed feelings about therapy. I knew it was necessary and I wanted to get my hand working normally as soon as possible but on the other hand I did wish it didn't hurt so terribly. Between therapy sessions twice a day, I moved my fingers slightly almost constantly. I also had a wooden dowel I tried to grasp. For some reason, my hand always felt cold. It wasn't cold to the touch, but it ached like your hand does when you stick it in ice water too long. It was the only part of me that ever felt cold.

Another painful part of treatment began about forty-eight hours after the accident. Before skin can be grafted to burned areas to replace the skin that has been destroyed, the damaged tissue has to be removed. The process is called debridement. There are several methods of debridement. The method we used employed an enzyme creme called Travase. The Travase was applied to the burned area, wet gauze placed over the wound, and the area wrapped in many layers of bandages. (Wrapping my hands, legs, and head in bandages helped to prevent swelling. It was also psychologically important to me that my wounds were covered. I felt I presented a much more acceptable appearance with all my wounds hidden by bandages.) As the wet gauze dried, the decayed tissue would adhere to it. When the dressings were removed, the decayed tissue was removed with them. My dressings were changed every six hours. The closer we got to the healthy tissue, the more painful the dressing changes became.

I did receive extra pain medication before dressing changes, but although it eased the pain somewhat, it did not remove it entirely. Dressing changes were as difficult for the nurses as they were for me. We all became good friends, and it is difficult to hurt someone you like even when you know it is necessary. I tried not to complain, although I did say "Ouch!" a lot, at varying decibels. The nurses were amused at my limited vocabulary. Apparently most patients turn the air blue with their swearing. Luckily for me, I'm not even tempted to anger God by swearing—I don't know how! I am so self-conscious using profanity it doesn't help me at all. Ouch! expressed my feelings better than anything else I could think of to say.

Most of the nurses were very gentle removing the dressings. One night, however, I had a new nurse—not just new to me, new to the burn unit. She had been told the best way to remove the dressings was quickly—you know, like ripping off adhesive tape quickly on the theory that the sooner it is off, the sooner the pain will stop. Well, when she removed the dressings from my legs I almost went through the ceiling. The next day I told everyone in sight what a terrible nurse I thought she was. I really misjudged her. She had simply been doing what she had been trained to do. Once she was told the procedure had to be varied according to the patient's tolerance, she became the gentlest of my nurses and a good friend.

One sign burned areas are ready for grafting is when they bleed when the dressings are changed. Dr. Morgan sounded a bit like a vampire to me when he would come in and say, "Did they bleed?" I had noticed he was never there during a dressing change, and I told him it was because he was a coward and couldn't stand to see me in pain. Boy, did he prove me wrong! Shortly before the burns were ready to graft, a point was reached where the Travase was no longer effectively dissolving the dead tissue and Dr. Morgan decided the wounds on my legs should be scraped. Yes, I did say scraped. It sounds horrible, and it was. Dr. Morgan came in and scraped the dead tissue off with a scalpel. Fortunately two nurses were present to hold my hands or I would have caused him to cut my leg off grabbing his hand to make him stop. It did the trick though, and soon my burns were ready to be grafted.

If you remember, earlier I said my hands were both elevated and bandaged. I should bring you up to date. I have told you my right hand was unbandaged and we were beginning therapy to make it work. Miraculously, my left hand had suffered only second-degree burns and healed without any grafting being necessary, except for one very small area at the base of my thumb. That spot of third-degree burns also healed itself, so after only ten days I was able to use my left hand. You don't know how wonderful it is to be able to feed yourself, to turn the pages of a book, to be able to push the button to ring for a nurse yourself. My brief period of being totally helpless really made me appreciate just how wonderful it is to be able to do things for myself. I thank the Lord I was helpless for those ten days. I not only learned what it is like to be totally dependent on others, I also learned how to accept help graciously. Often the most wonderful gift you can give a friend or a loved one is to allow that person to help. I might still be withholding that gift if I had not been forced to accept help from others.

Have you ever thought it would be terrible to have to use a bedpan all the time? Believe me, there was a time I prefered a bedpan to getting out of bed. After several days, the catheter and the I.V. were removed. I had been lying around long enough, Dr. Morgan decided and gave orders that I should get up and walk to the bathroom. It was about three feet from my bed but it seemed like a mile. At first the nurses were told to put my back brace on before I got up. I wish you could have seen us. It was like a scene from a slapstick comedy. First they would put on my brace—an awkward procedure when I was lying down. Then I would swing my legs over the edge of the bed; pause while the blood flowed into my lower legs, making them throb horribly; and, with the help of two nurses, stand up and hobble those three feet to the bathroom. A footstool was made out of an upsidedown trash can covered with towels so I could raise my legs while I was on the "throne." Sometimes by the time I sat down I had almost forgotten why I wanted to get up. Eventually we were permitted to leave my back brace off when I was only up for my brief journey to the "john." I knew I was getting better when it only took one nurse to help me back and forth. After 10 P.M. I was no longer required to get up. I have never been so glad to see 10 P.M. arrive as I was those days.

For over two weeks I had been given only sponge baths. My hair had not been washed and was full of dirt, dried blood, and medication from my bandages. I guess it really looked a mess. It didn't bother me; I never had to look at it since it was always covered with bandages. The nurses had to look at it, though, when they changed my dressings. One nurse, Linda, really wanted to wash my hair and would ask Dr. Morgan each day when he was going to let her wash it.

Finally, on December 21, exactly three weeks after the accident, Dr. Morgan came in and asked, "How would you like to take a shower?"

I was horrified. "That's a terrible idea. How are you

going to keep the water off the burned areas? It sounds painful."

For the first time in our relationship, Dr. Morgan raised his voice. "Don't you think we know how to do these things?"

Actually he knew it would be painful to shower, but it was necessary. A yellow-petroleum-impregnated gauze called Xeroform had been used as part of the dressings, and the residue which clung to the undamaged area of my skin had to be washed off. In my first shower the water rolled off me like a duck. The water did hurt when it hit my burns but the spray was gentle and it wasn't as unbearable as I had feared. Linda helped me take my showers and finally got a chance to wash my hair. It did feel good to get my hair clean. I think it took three showers to get all the dirt out of my hair. Fortunately, my hair had not burned. It was slightly frizzled around the hair line but that was all.

It sounds as if I was always in pain. I wasn't. As long as I was lying quietly in bed I was comfortable—more comfortable than I would have thought possible. Only during dressing changes and therapy and on my brief excursions out of bed did I experience intense pain. Out of twenty-four hours a day I was in pain no more than four or five. Even a sissy like me can handle that.

I sincerely believe I experienced much less pain than most burn patients. I know Dr. Morgan tried to use procedures that would be as painless as possible. I know I was receiving pain medication, but I also know that the Lord was honoring his promise to protect me from pain. I had told him I can't take much pain, and he saw to it that I had no more than I could handle.

Even during the more than usually painful weeks preparing the burns for grafting there was one part of treatment I really enjoyed. Eating! I have always enjoyed eating. Burn patients need almost three times the normal amount of calories. It was really great to eat everything in sight without worrying about gaining weight. Sometimes patients don't feel like eating, but Dr. Morgan never had that problem with me. At meals it was hard for the kitchen to get all my food on the tray. Even hospital food tasted good. (Except the bread. The bread was horrible. I would take a bite and the more I chewed it the larger it seemed to grow, until it was almost impossible to swallow it. After one or two attempts to eat it I gave up. I never ordered bread, but if the kitchen sent it by mistake, that is one thing I left on my tray.)

At last the day came for grafting—December 24, Christmas Eve. When burns are ready to be grafted, the operation must be done within a short period of time to achieve the best results. I'm sure Dr. Morgan could have performed the surgery on the 23rd or the 26th, but I believe he chose to do it on Christmas Eve to make my first Christmas without my family easier for me. Still fuzzy from the anesthetic, I was almost unaware that Christmas had passed.

The first few days after surgery I had to remain in bed. When I was told I could get up and take a short walk accompanied by one of the nurses, I wondered if it would still be painful to stand. It wasn't. Do you have any idea how wonderful it is to be able to stand, to walk without pain? I now understand some of the suffering experienced by those with chronic illnesses like arthritis. I praise the Lord my days of pain were short. The first day out of bed I was shaky and could walk only a short distance, but it was great!

After new skin had been grafted to my legs and face,

we began debriding my fingertips so that they could be regrafted. I amazed my nurses—and myself—by learning to remove the dressings by myself and pull off the dead tissue with a pair of tweezers. Normally I am very squeamish. Bruce even had to remove splinters from our kids' fingers because I couldn't bring myself to do it. The real reason I became involved in doing the debriding myself was because it was less painful that way. I knew exactly when to stop. Doing this was also a lesson for me that the Lord can give me strength to perform any task he deems necessary.

Soon it was time to cover those fingertips with skin again. This time the grafts took completely. Praise the Lord! I was now totally free from pain except during therapy, and even that was less difficult to endure. Many patients experience much pain from their donor sites while those areas which have given a split thickness of their skin to be grafted onto the burned area are healing. My donor sites were never painful. They did itch, but they did not hurt.

I did not see my face until a month after the accident. Dr. Morgan worried that I was not more anxious to see what I looked like. I wasn't afraid to see myself; I just didn't want to see myself at my worst. I felt Dr. Morgan would know when the time was right.

"How would you like to go to a beauty shop to have your hair done?" he asked one day.

I thought it a rather funny idea to get my hair done and then wrap it back up in bandages. But it would be fun to get out of the hospital even for a short time. When I said, "Great!" my sister, Jo Ann, who was at the hospital with me during that time, was immediately assigned the task of purchasing clothes for me to wear. She found a beautiful brown pants suit and a white imitation leather jacket. Tennis shoes completed the outfit. The appointment was made for January 2. I had arrived at the hospital December 2 at 1:30 A.M. I had not been outside for a month. The cold, fresh air felt great. At the beauty shop I was seated in front of a mirror and Dr. Morgan removed my bandages. It was a sneaky way to get me to see myself, but it worked. I was surprised at how good I looked. Not great, but much better than I expected. (I have recently seen a picture taken about that time. I thought I looked better than I did.) Being prepared for the worst, I saw myself through rose-colored glasses. Dr. Morgan breathed a sigh of relief.

After I had been in the hospital about five weeks I was moved from my room in the intensive care unit to a room across the hall. Dr. Morgan felt I was getting spoiled by the constant attention of the nurses. I suspect he also thought I was getting to know too much about the inner workings of the hospital, eavesdropping on the nurses at the nursing station across from my room. The new room to which I was moved was much more attractive than the room in ICU. That room had pale cream-colored walls. The only outside window, at the head of my bed, was so high I could not see out of it. The room was also very small and crowded. My new room was more spacious, with a large window looking out onto a tree-shaded patio. One wall was covered with brightly flowered wallpaper that seemed beautiful to me. Dr. Morgan did not share my enthusiasm. "That wallpaper will surely shorten the time your visitors stay," he predicted.
He was wrong. It didn't.

My new room was supposed to be connected with the nurses' station in ICU, but because of some kind of electrician's foul-up, to contact the nurses I had to use the phone. That would have been fine, but the phone was always busy. Fortunately, they checked on me frequently, and at the same time I learned to be more self-sufficient. I admit I did miss not being the center of attention.

The first night in my new room, while I was feeling very sorry for myself, the patient in the next room came by to chat. She was an older woman and had just had a mastectomy. The operation had been successful, and although it had only been performed a day or two before, she could already raise her arm almost normally. Despite all that, she was really feeling sorry for herself too.

Not in the mood to sympathize, I told her she could count her blessings; her deformity would not be noticeable when she was clothed. I would always have scars which showed, and not only had I been burned and scarred, I told her, but I had also lost my family. She left feeling sorrier for me than for herself.

After she left, I really felt guilty. I really shouldn't have been so hard on her, I thought.

The next morning one of the nurses came in and asked me what I had said to the woman. The nurse had noticed she was no longer full of self-pity and was in better spirits than at any time since she had been admitted. The Lord had even used my bad humor, my self-pity, in a positive way to help someone else.

I was beginning to make myself at home in my new room when Dr. Morgan surprised me. One Friday, January 16, people began dropping by my room to say good-by. Good-by? According to the timetable I had originally been given, I should have another five or six weeks in the hospital. Dr. Morgan had told me I could leave the hospital that weekend to have dinner with friends but that was all.

That evening Dr. Morgan came in. "Why does everyone think I am leaving?" I asked.

"Because you are," he said. "I thought you might like to move to the Holiday Inn."

I was shocked. "But I'm not ready to leave the hospital. I'd planned on being here three months."

"If you don't like the Holiday Inn I'll let you come back," he promised.

I was about to leave my cocoon and reenter the world.

- 5 -

LETTERS, VISITORS, LOVE, AND LONELINESS

I had told the Lord I couldn't cope with the loneliness of being a widow and being childless. Have you ever tried to be lonely in the intensive care unit of a hospital? It's impossible. The Lord could not have put me in a better place. When Jim, Virginia, and I arrived at Chico there were only two beds in the burn unit, both in the same room. Dr. Morgan felt Jim and Virginia should be together so I was given a room in the intensive care unit. At Chico Community Memorial Hospital the nursing staff of the burn unit, ICU, and the coronary care unit are trained to work in all three areas, so my being in a room in ICU presented no problems for the staff.

It was great for me! Not only was my room directly across from the nurses station so I could keep track of their activities, it was the first room in ICU. Everyone coming to visit other patients had to pass my room. Once I was out of isolation, all the ministers coming to visit critically ill patients on the unit also began stopping

by my room on the way out. They said visiting me
cheered them up. Whatever their reasons, they ministered to my needs as well.

A sign outside my door said:

Visiting Limited to Family Members

Five Minutes per Visit

Fortunately no one paid any attention to that sign. Our
neighbors the Le Fevres were on their way home from
Dunsmuir when they learned of the accident, and they
came to Chico to be with the Dixons and with me. We
had attended a small mission church in Dunsmuir—St.
Barnabas—and Father Torgerson, the pastor there,
followed us down the mountain to minister to our needs
and also to comfort and console our friends and
relatives as they arrived.

The day after the accident my husband's partners,
Bill Peck and Jim Loebl, and my sister, Jo Ann Melvin,
arrived. Bill and Jim were a great help in handling the
funeral arrangements and all the legal formalities
attending a death, and in taking care of all my bills.
They also found a lovely woman, Hazel Fulkerson, to
live in my house and care for it while I was in Chico. All
I had to worry about was getting well. I think one of the
funniest sights I have ever seen was the sight of 6'4" Jim
Loebl trying to don a surgical gown, mask, cap, and
gloves to come in to see me. (Infection is an ever-present
danger in burn injuries, so until all the grafting was
completed, everyone visiting me had to wear sterile
surgical gowns, masks, caps, and gloves.) Jim just could
not get the mask on right until finally a nurse stood on a
chair and put it on for him.

Bill said he had worried all the way to Chico about
how he would respond if, when he walked in, I said,

"Bill, I don't want to live. I have nothing to live for." Instead, when he came into my room, grasped my shoulder—about the only exposed part of me, and said, "Everything will be all right, Diane," I answered, "I know it will, Bill." He walked out of the room feeling ten feet tall.

I know everyone who came to visit me was worried about what they should say to me—worried whether they should mention Bruce or the kids; in fact, whether they should even talk about their own children. Really, that was not necessary; I was comforted by their mere presence. I knew how difficult it would have been for me to pluck up the courage to visit a friend in the hospital who had lost her family and who was badly injured, so I tried to set my friends at ease. I would talk about Bruce and the children, and, even at the beginning, enjoy remembering our good times together. When I would also encourage them to talk about their families, you could almost see them breathe a sigh of relief. They could relax once they knew they did not have to avoid mentioning my family or theirs.

One of the first ways the accident was used by the Lord for good in my life was to strengthen the love I have for my sister. My only sister, Jo Ann is a beautiful girl. She is three years younger than I am and several inches taller (I am 5'2"; she is 5'8"), having passed me by when she was four and I was seven. She has gorgeous red hair, while mine is naturally light brown. Few people, seeing us for the first time, would believe we are sisters.

There was a great deal of rivalry between us as we were growing up. As the oldest, I thought I should be able to tell her what to do. As the biggest, she told me.

In many ways she was at a disadvantage. People often forgot she was three years younger than I and expected her to be able to do all the things I could do and to act my age. After we grew up and married we saw each other only occasionally, usually on holidays. It has been wonderful to discover what a capable, compassionate woman Jo Ann has become. She was with me almost constantly the first five weeks I was in the hospital. I will be forever grateful to her husband, Dan, for allowing her to stay with me. I am also grateful to her mother-in-law, Gert Melvin, whose help freed Jo Ann to be with me.

During my waking hours, Jo Ann remained in my room with me almost constantly, except when she was chased out by the nurses so they could bathe me or change my dressings. Jo Ann was the ideal hospital visitor. She had the ability just to be there when that was what I needed. Often I did not want to talk and simply needed to have someone with me to prevent loneliness from overwhelming me. If I did want to talk, she talked with me. If I wanted to watch TV, she watched TV with me. When I was unable to use my hands, she rang the buzzer for the nurse when I needed one, and she helped feed me my meals.

Having to be fed, I certainly developed a lot of sympathy for babies. No matter how hard the person feeding you tries, he or she always seems to feed you too fast or too slow or to give you the food in the wrong order. It was great when I could feed myself, though even after I could use a fork and a spoon, I still needed help cutting my food. It is impossible to cut meat using one hand. Try it. Jo Ann proved most adept at cutting.

Jo Ann also proved her merits as a private secretary. I

was lucky. My tragedy made the headlines. People all over California knew I needed love and prayers. As far away as Hong Kong, friends knew of the accident the next day, and the response was unbelievable. I received cards and letters from over three hundred people, many from people I did not know. Some were friends of Bruce's, but many were from strangers who read of the accident and wrote to say they cared. Many Christians also wrote that they were praying for me. Prayer groups all over the state were lifting me up in prayer. A priest at one of the Catholic churches in Ventura—Sacred Heart—mentioned me in the prayers at his church for so long that someone finally asked him if I was a Catholic. He responded, "No, but what difference does that make?" I think one of the most wonderful developments of recent years is that Christians of all denominations have finally come to realize that our similarities are more important than our differences. The important thing is that we all worship the same God and we all believe in Jesus as our Lord and Savior.

I wanted to respond to all the wonderful friends, new and old, who wrote to me. Since I could not hold a pen or pencil, Jo Ann would write the letters for me as I dictated them to her. It was the only time in my life my correspondence was up to date. You cannot know how much all those letters and cards and prayers meant to me. Before the accident I often wanted to write to friends who were ill or who had lost a loved one, but I hesitated because I did not know what to say. I found it is not what is said that is important. To me what counted was that all those wonderful people cared enough to write. If all you send is a blank paper with two words on it, *I care*, that is enough.

There were some who did not write because they could not put their feelings into words. I understood. I knew they were not silent because they were uncaring, but because they cared so much.

Rereading some of the cards and letters I received, I am reminded once again how much love was sent my way. Many letters mention constant phone calls between Chico and Ventura and from one home to another. The telephone lines were really kept busy. The nurses later told me the first two days I was in the hospital one nurse was kept busy almost full time answering the phone and giving the latest information on my condition and on the Dixons'. I had a phone in my room for a couple of days, but when I found I did not have the energy to talk to many callers, the phone was removed until I was stronger.

On days I felt alone, on days I felt like giving up, the Lord would remind me of the hundreds of people who were praying for my recovery, of all the friends who were writing, and I would know I was not alone. I couldn't give up. I couldn't let them down.

Not only was my sister writing letters for me, friends in Ventura were also busy writing letters in my behalf. Dottie Loebl and Edie LeFevre sent cards of thanks to all those involved in the rescue. Much to my surprise, I later found that the brave men on the rescue teams are seldom thanked. I cannot understand how anyone can fail to thank the men who have risked their own lives to rescue people in distress.

On Jim Loebl's first visit to the hospital, he said everyone in Ventura was asking what they could do to help. I suggested a clean-up crew be recruited to empty out my refrigerator. We had left for Dunsmuir the day after Thanksgiving, and I had just shoved all the leftovers in the refrigerator. When I could think about such things again, I had visions of everything turning green. It was done.

Neighbors, the Eulaus, took our springer spaniel to their home and cared for him until I returned to Ventura. Rachel Stauffer fed our cats—three adults and three kittens—until Mrs. Fulkerson moved into the house. Many friends wondered if it wouldn't be best for them to remove Bruce's clothing and belongings and the children's things from the house so I wouldn't have to go through them when I got home. I assured Jim that when I died I would do my best to return and haunt anyone who removed anything belonging to Bruce or the children from the house. I knew even then that a house devoid of any trace of my loved ones would be a truly empty house.

Because I was very weak the first few weeks, only a few friends were encouraged to visit, but visit they did. Bud and Sally Hartman, partners in our plane, came and brought with them Dale and Peg Armstrong. As I have mentioned, Dale is a plastic surgeon. I am sure one reason he came to visit was so he could give a report to my friends on the quality of the medical care I was receiving. After viewing my right hand when the bandages were removed, he wrote me from Ventura to praise the care I was receiving from Dr. Morgan. Dr. Herb Hamel and Bill Ahern, flying buddies of Bruce, also flew up to visit. My uncle, Noah Purcell, who lives in Texas, was visiting California at the time of the accident and was able to come to Chico. Not having seen him for several years, I was sorry he had to see me in bed with my head swathed in bandages looking rather like a large pumpkin, but I was glad he came, just the same.

Christmas was approaching. Dr. Morgan sings in the choir at St. John's Episcopal Church, and he brought the choir to serenade the Dixons and me. As I was still in isolation, my door was supposed to remain closed. But with the door closed, it was impossible to hear the choir. It was fortunate for me that Dr. Morgan was there to open it so I could enjoy the beautiful Christmas music. The nurses would have been very hesitant to do so, because Dr. Morgan really jumps them if sterile conditions are not maintained. One of the hospital staff, Kurt Cessna, even dressed up as Santa Claus and delivered roses to all the women patients. He made a very jolly Santa. If you have to be in the hospital at Christmas, Chico Community Memorial Hospital is a good place to be.

On Christmas Day Jo Ann's family came up from Long Beach. A day room was set aside for our use, and I was wheeled in on my bed. Fortunately, it was no longer necessary for me to be in isolation, and though I was still somewhat groggy from surgery the day before I do remember we had a lovely dinner together—turkey with all the trimmings, even pumpkin and mince pie. Not quite as good as home cooking of course, but the best the hospital kitchen could turn out. After we opened gifts together, I returned to my room. One gift I really appreciated was an AM-FM radio from Bill Peck.

It was great to see Jo Ann's kids and to spend Christmas with her family. Jo Ann's children are older than mine; that Christmas Dennis was almost sixteen, Donald almost fifteen, and Deanna was twelve.

New Year's Eve saw another celebration in the hospital. The nurses decorated my room with a big Happy New Year's sign. Individual letters were cut out and strung across my room on traction ropes. (Fortunately no one in the unit was in traction.) Also among the decorations were balloons pilfered from the emergency room where they are kept for children who might be brought in. There were all colors—red, yellow, blue, orange. The atmosphere was really festive. Champagne was even brought to my room at midnight. I couldn't stay awake but I had told the nurses ahead of time I would rather have a champagne breakfast on New Year's Day, and I did.

After accompanying me on my trip to the beauty shop, Jo Ann had to return home to Long Beach. She had stayed with me over a month, and her family needed her. After Jo Ann left, other friends planned their visits so I would always have company. Bruce's cousin Bonnie Robie and her husband, Wally, came up for three days and brought a ceramic elf their son Jason had painted for me. Bonnie and Jason had spent two weeks with the children and me at our lake cabin in Minnesota the previous summer and Jason had really idolized Scott. I can still see Jason trailing after Scott, who was six years older. It was Scott's first opportunity to play big brother and he had thoroughly enjoyed it. As Scott's mother I held a special place in Jason's heart. Bonnie, too, proved to be a good secretary.

When Marcia Drescher and Carolyn Bertelson also came to visit, I was allowed to leave the hospital to go to lunch with them—my first meal away from the hospital. We went to a restaurant called Mike and Eddies. The food was served buffet style, and my biggest treat came when I reached the carver at the end of the line—a slice of *rare* roast beef, something you just don't get in the hospital. Delicious! Marcia and Carolyn are long-time friends. Their husbands were also attorneys, and we had first become friends when Bruce, Phil, and Karl were all working in the Ventura D.A.'s office. It was great to see them. The "care package" of homemade goodies they brought was especially appreciated.

In referring to the way people responded to my needs, I think Jim Loebl said it all. The accident really renewed his faith in people, he said. I have found people do respond when they know there is a need. Unfortunately, many of us try so hard to handle our own problems that not only do we fail to ask the Lord's help, we do not even allow our friends the privilege of sharing our burdens.

-6-

PUT ON A HAPPY FACE

Many of the nurses worried that I did not seem to be grieving, that I seldom cried. The nurses on the night shift (from 11:00 P.M. to 7:00 A.M.) did not worry. Late at night when all was quiet and I was alone I allowed the tears to flow. I knew all my friends and my family were also grieving and suffering for me and with me. I wanted them to know I would be all right. When they were with me I "put on a happy face."

I told no one but the priests who visited me—Father Henry, Father Torgerson, and Father Sturni—about seeing and talking to the Lord on the mountain. I told others I knew God would take care of me but I did not reveal the source of my faith. I was sure most people would think I had been hallucinating. I did not want them to worry that I was losing my mind.

Rereading many of the letters I received, I am once again made aware how strong everyone thought I was. I was not strong enough to cope with the tragedy of the accident, but I knew the Lord would provide the strength I needed. In fact, when Father Sturni first came to visit me, having been told by Dr. Morgan that I was in the hospital and needed his pastoral care, he said, "I want to assure you God is with you."

He was pleased but astonished at my response. "Yes, I know." Although I did not tell Father Sturni at that first meeting the source of my faith, he did become the first person I told. I often complained to Father Sturni that I wished people would stop commenting on my strength because I was really weak. Still, I admit that it was important to me that everyone think I was strong, and I fostered their belief in my strength.

I am thankful I was seriously injured in the plane crash. Coping with my own injuries helped me adjust to the loss of my family. The first few weeks I was in the hospital it took all of my strength and energy to heal *me*. If I was to live I had to concentrate on that, and there was no energy left over to grieve. Certainly, I was aware Bruce and my three children were dead, but I did not dwell on my loss. By the time I was strong enough to allow myself to grieve, to fully comprehend my loss, that loss had gradually become a part of me. The shock of my family's death was not nearly as great as it would have been had I escaped the accident uninjured.

My injuries helped me in a practical way too. If you have ever tried to cry with your head completely swathed in bandages, you know that it is very uncomfortable to lie around in wet dressings. Before the burns on my left hand healed, it was even more uncomfortable, because I couldn't even wipe my own nose. Now I should tell you that I am a person who plans ahead. I knew my dressings were changed every six hours. If I felt like crying just after a dressing change, I would put it off. I would think, "I don't want to lie here with wet dressings, so I will cry just before the next dressing change." Of course, the Lord knew what I was doing, and, inevitably, before the next dressing change something would happen to lift my spirits. I would have a special visitor, receive a stack of letters, or perhaps open the Bible to a Scripture verse that spoke to my need. One such verse was John 3:16: For God so loved the world that he gave his only Son, that whoever believes in him [my family] should not perish but have eternal life. By the time I had planned to cry I no longer felt like crying.

Sometimes in the middle of the night I did let the tears flow. "Why me, Lord?" I would cry. "Why did you take my wonderful family? I loved them so much." I knew deep within myself that God had not caused the accident, but I think in times of trouble or sorrow, we all cry, "Why me?"

At those times the Lord really spoke to me. "Christian death is not the worst thing that can happen, Diane," he reminded me. "In fact, death is the perfect healing. There is no pain and suffering in heaven."

When I would ask, "Why couldn't they have lived?" he would say, "Diane, would you really want them to be alive even if they were suffering, if they were permanently disabled, if they had sustained brain damage? Wouldn't you rather have the assurance that they are in heaven with me? If you do believe that through my death and resurrection all who believe in me and claim me as savior have everlasting life, a life full of joy, are you not being selfish when you fail to rejoice for them?"

I would be forced to admit that I am glad they are in heaven. I am glad they did not suffer. My grief was for myself, not for them. I grieved they were no longer alive to give me pleasure. I did rejoice they were with the Lord.

If Bruce or one of the children had escaped the accident without being badly injured, they would still have suffered tremendously. As pilot of the plane, Bruce might not have been able to deal with the feelings of guilt that would have assailed him had he survived the crash and lost his children, or had he survived and watched me suffer. The accident was not his fault, but he would have blamed himself.

In fact, at first I blamed him too. I was very angry with him. I knew we both believed it was safe to take off that fatal afternoon but I needed to blame someone. My anger helped me to cope with my loss, because first I really only grieved for my children. After I had worked through my grief for them, then I was able to release my anger at Bruce and grieve for him. My children were so close to one another and we were so happy as a family, I am glad none of them had to experience the grief of losing a parent or a brother or sister. I am glad they are still together.

After the accident, my minister, Father Robert Henry, came to Chico to visit me and to plan the funeral. In the Episcopal church, all burials are conducted from the church. I requested a memorial fund be established in memory of Bruce, Scott, Mary, and Laura, and that funds donated be used for the endowment fund of the parish day school. The day of the funeral I was thankful I am a member of a liturgical church. All our services are in our prayer book including the burial service. During the funeral, while lying in my bed in Chico five hundred miles away, I was able to read the service in the prayer book while it was taking place in Ventura. I had a sense of participation in my family's funeral that would not have been possible otherwise.

Friends wrote to tell me the funeral was beautiful and dignified, the church full of friends including many children who were friends of Scott, Mary, and Laura. It was a beautiful day. The sun was shining brightly. One friend wrote, "The enormity of the tragedy was horribly and obviously impressed upon us by the presence of the four caskets." Closing his letter, he continued, "We as his [Bruce's] friends are diminished by his death. And yet to dwell on that is an inappropriate placement of emphasis. It is better we emphasize the way in which we were enriched for having associated with Bruce."

It was really unnecessary for the funeral to be described to me. I felt as if I had been present. Memorial gifts came pouring in from hundreds of friends and relatives. Over $6,000 was contributed to the memorial fund in memory of my family. Once again friends in Ventura came forward to help, sending the necessary thank-you notes in my behalf for the generous contributions.

Resolutions honoring Bruce were passed by the Board of Supervisors of Ventura County, the City Councils of Ventura and of Ojai, and the Greater Ventura Chamber of Commerce, but the most meaningful tribute was a statement made by one of the pallbearers (I have never known which one) who said of Bruce, "He was a guy who brought a lot of joy into a lot of people's lives." Knowing my grief was shared by so many helped to ease the pain.

The Christmas season was rapidly approaching.

Television ads and programs were filled with children joyfully anticipating Christmas. Sometimes one of the children would remind me of Scott, of Mary, or of Laura, and the tears would well up.

Christmas is a special family time but, more important, it is the anniversary of Jesus' birth. Christmas 1976 was a very special time for me—a time for grief but also a time for joy. Because Christ was born and died for our sins on the cross I was able to rejoice. Remembering that God so loved me that he gave his son to die for me and for my husband and children so that we could all have the promise of everlasting life was beautiful. As I thought about Jesus' birth, about his death, about his resurrection, I remembered that God too knows what it is to lose a child. He watched his own son suffer on a cross and die. Even though he knew his son would conquer death and rise again to dwell with him in glory, still he must have grieved for him.

I am lucky. My children died, but as painful as it is to lose a child to death, how much more painful it is to have a child reject you. To say, "So you're my mother, so what? I don't need you!" Not only did God give his son to die for us on the cross, he also suffers the daily pain of having his own children, his creation, reject him and deny his existence. I would not compare myself to God in any way, but I know he loves all of us and I know his suffering when we turn away from him, his grief over his lost children, makes my grief insignificant.

God used the wonderful staff of the hospital to relieve my pain and heal my body. He used my many friends to ease the loneliness of my days in the hospital. He himself healed my grief. He was beginning to turn my mourning into joy.

- 7 -

OUT OF THE COCOON

Fresh air! It was wonderful to step out of the hospital into the fresh air. Amazingly I can't remember the weather on that momentous day. I only remember how good it felt to be out of the hospital. Good, but also frightening. I had been out of the hospital briefly on only two occasions since December 1. How would people react to my bandages? Would I be able to survive when I was not surrounded by the caring staff of the hospital?

Two friends from my church in Ventura, Linda Barthuli and Ann Bachhuber were in Chico when I was released. It took all three of us to move my things to the Holiday Inn. I had accumulated quite a few belongings during my stay in the hospital. I was given a room which adjoined the Dixons' room. I would need their help.

After I settled in, Ann, Linda, and I went to the nearby shopping center to outfit me. I had plenty of nightgowns and robes but I had only one outfit to wear out (the pants suit, tennis shoes, and jacket my sister had purchased for me when Dr. Morgan took me to the beauty shop). We did find two pants suits that would fit over my back brace—a blue one and a green one. Trying them on was something. Linda had to help me dress and undress and, to say the least, it was an awkward process getting the slacks up under the brace and easing my still tender right hand through the sleeves. At least we didn't have to worry about messing up my hair. It was still covered with bandages except for a pony tail sticking up through the top. Fortunately, the night of the accident, Virginia had grabbed my purse thinking it was hers, so I had my credit cards and driver's license.

When we returned to the Holiday Inn, I rested while Ann and Linda hemmed my new pants. Being only 5′2″, I never seem to be able to find pants that are the right length. I love shopping but I found just a couple of hours really tired me out. It would be a long time before I fully recovered my strength.

We went out together for dinner that night. Not fancy, but it really hit the spot. We had *pizza*. It tasted great! We finished the evening back at the Holiday Inn watching a hilarious British comedy show on TV. I don't think I have ever laughed harder. Part of my enjoyment of that show may have come from the exhilarating feeling of being out of the hospital. Part of the enjoyment came from spending that very important evening with two wonderful friends.

Ann and Linda left to go to their room. Suddenly, I was overwhelmed with loneliness. Being in a motel room reminded me of the wonderful trips Bruce and I had taken and of the wonderful trips we took together as a family. I could remember trying to find room for a crib or later a rollaway bed after Laura arrived. I remember the girls' comments when they slept together in a double bed. "Mommy, I can't sleep. Laura is tickling me." "No, I'm not," says Laura. "Mary is bothering me!" and on and on until Bruce or I would get angry and tell them to keep quiet. I suddenly realized that I had never spent the night alone in a motel room before.

Just as I was beginning to be overwhelmed by my memories and by my loneliness—as if in answer to my unspoken prayer—the phone rang. It was Dr. Morgan. I don't know if he knew the Lord was prompting him to call. "I thought you might be lonely. So I called to ask, how do you like the Holiday Inn?"

"It's fine to have some freedom, but, in all honesty, there are some ways I prefer being in the hospital. Somebody would be waiting on me hand and foot," I admitted.

"That's one reason I thought you should leave the hospital."

After our conversation I was able to get a good night's sleep. The next morning after breakfast Ann and Linda had to say good-by and return to Ventura. I was really alone.

Well, not quite alone. The Dixons were with me.

Before the accident, Jim and Virginia were only casual friends. The first few weeks after the accident I avoided seeing them even though we were in the same hospital. I could hardly bring myself to ask the nurses and our mutual friends about them. I blamed myself that they were in the hospital. It had been my suggestion that they accompany us on our visit to the LeFevres. I *knew* it was not my fault. I certainly had had no premonitions of disaster, but still I did feel guilty.

Fortunately, the Dixons did not blame me. In fact, it was Virginia who came to visit me in the hospital once she was allowed to leave their room. The first few days we were in the Holiday Inn Virginia was a big help. She would come to my room each morning to help me dress. My back brace tightened on the right side and I could not fasten it with my right hand. I soon learned to do it lefthanded even though it was somewhat awkward, but even when I could dress myself, I still needed the Dixons' help to open my door. In order to unlock my door, it was necessary to pull the door handle toward me with one hand while turning the key with the other—a maneuver I couldn't quite manage. Jim and Virginia proved most adept at opening the door for me. When they weren't available I had to ask someone from the front desk to come up with me and unlock the door.

Strangely enough, most of the doors in the Holiday Inn opened with just a turn of the key. Is it possible that the Lord was still teaching me to accept help graciously?

Jim and Virginia's son brought them their car so we had transportation. We usually went to the hospital for our dressing changes and to Dr. Morgan's for our periodic checkups together. It was also necessary for me to go to my therapist's office daily for therapy. If it was convenient, Jim and Virginia would take me. Other times I would take a taxi. Once I regained my strength, I often walked. Being out in the fresh air felt good, and it was just about a mile from the Holiday Inn to O. D.'s office. The Dixons and I usually ate dinner together, and, much to our amazement, we found Chico had several good restaurants. Often there was a wait, as only one of the restaurants would accept reservations; but one look at Virginia and me, our heads still in bandages, usually resulted in seats being found almost immediately.

My bandages covered my entire head. You could see only my eyes, my mouth, and the tip of my nose. Virginia's bandages made her look like a nun, encircling her head but leaving her face exposed. Those bandages and, later, when we began wearing them, our masks also caused other drivers to be very courteous.

When we were in the car, Virginia and I were always in the front seat. Jim was under orders from Dr. Morgan to keep his leg raised whenever possible, so he sat in back where he could put his leg up. Any time Virginia was waiting to make a left turn, drivers traveling the opposite direction would yield so she could turn. I don't know if they were being nice to two invalids or if we looked so strange they were afraid of us. I will always be grateful to the Dixons for not blaming me for their plight and for stretching out the hand of friendship to me.

Shortly after our release from the hospital, Jim and Virginia celebrated their seventh wedding anniversary. Friends of theirs had come to Chico from Ventura and from Oroville to help them celebrate. Dr. Morgan and his wife, Kay, had been invited, as had Father Sturni. The three of them were unable to join us for dinner because St. John's choir was having a birthday party for Father Sturni that evening; but they did join us in the Dixons' room for a few moments before dinner. It was my night to show off. For Christmas Dr. Morgan had given me a bottle of wine and had said that when I could lift the bottle with my right hand and give it to him he

would give me a special reward. I had finally progressed
to the point that I could grasp the neck of the now-
empty bottle and hold it aloft long enough to hand it to
someone. When Dr. Morgan knocked at the door, I
opened it and with my right hand handed him the
empty bottle.

"You were supposed to hand it to me full," he said.
Nevertheless, he was pleased with my progress. I should
add that I never received the promised reward so
maybe the bottle was supposed to be full.

It was while I was in the Holiday Inn I first began to
be attacked by bouts of loneliness. A motel room is often
a lonely, impersonal place. It was in the Holiday Inn
that I once again began experiencing the Lord's
presence in a very special way. When I was lonely I
would pray to him and remind him he had promised to
take care of my loneliness, one of the three specific
areas I had told him I would need special help with that
night on Black Butte. I don't always pray fancy prayers
in King James English. Often I would just turn to him
and say, "Lord, you promised you would help me cope
with this loneliness. Help! in Jesus' name, Amen."

The help was always there. If it was a reasonable
hour, the phone would often ring and I would know I
was not alone. But since my prayers were often prayed
in the wee hours of the morning when it is hard for God
to convince any of us we should wake up and call a
friend, he often ministered to me directly. I haven't
seen him again and I don't think I will in this earthly
life; but I often feel his presence. It is just as if he is in
the room with me, holding me and saying, "It's all right,
Diane, you are not alone. I'm here."

I know he is with me in those hours of need. I believe

that one of the most wonderful results of Jesus' death, resurrection, and ascension into heaven is that once he ascended into heaven, he sent the Holy Spirit to be with all Christians all the time. It must have been wonderful to walk the earth with Jesus, to listen to him teach, and to witness the miracles he performed. But when Jesus was on earth he was not only fully divine, he was also fully human, and, like any human, he could only be in one place at one time. Now, through the power of the Holy Spirit, he is not limited by time or space but can be with us all everywhere. In my times of loneliness he taught me that truth.

When I was released from the hospital, I wondered how people would react to my bandages. I had found that my bandages assured me of extra consideration. It was obvious I had been badly injured and everyone was sympathetic. I was about to embark on a new phase of treatment. I was about to begin wearing my Jobst garments. These are special elastic garments, made to measure, which exert a constant pressure on the grafted areas and on donor sites so that they heal smoothly. Burn scars often contract while they are healing. Unfortunately, my skin also tends to form raised hypertrophic or keloid scars, even on donor sites. The Jobst garments helped my skin grafts heal smoothly and retarded the formation of raised scars on most of my donor sites.

My Jobst garments arrived a couple weeks after I was released from the hospital. I had a mask that covered my whole head, similar to a ski mask, with holes for my eyes, ears, nose, and mouth. Worn with a head scarf tied in back, it made me look like the town bank robber. Without a scarf I looked like a Martian. I also had a vest that zippered up the front and a pair of stockings rather like panty hose but without toes. Gloves for my hands completed the ensemble. I wore all the garments twenty-four hours a day, except my left glove, which I wore only at night, and my mask, which I removed when I ate. The first week or ten days I was out of my "get-up" about three hours a day. At first I had only one set of garments, and they had to be washed daily. That gave me three hours of freedom.

It was difficult sleeping in what amounted to a full body girdle. The only time I took sleeping pills after my release from the hospital was the first four nights I wore my Jobst suit. Since I was accustomed to sleeping in loose nightgowns, it was really difficult to sleep in those tight garments. Because I was more comfortable sleeping out of them, I would wake up about 4:00 A.M., take them off, rinse them out, hang them to dry, and then crawl back in bed and luxuriate in comfort until about 7:00 or 8:00 A.M.

Getting dressed was quite a process. My right hand was still not strong enough or mobile enough to be much help pulling up those tight stockings, so I eased them on inch by inch, using my left hand to pull them up. At first that probably took me about twenty minutes. Later I got much faster. I couldn't work the zipper on my vest by myself. Have you ever tried to close a separating zipper on a tight elastic garment one-handed? It doesn't work. Virginia helped me into my vest until I got smart and learned to unzip it only half way and then pull it off and on over my head. Then I could dress myself again. I was still wearing my back brace and it went on over my vest and stockings. Quite a set of underwear.

When my mask arrived I had my hair cut short. One advantage to wearing a Jobst mask is that you don't have to worry about your hair or your makeup. I did wear lipstick and eye shadow but my hair and the rest of my face were hidden. Much to my surprise, my mask did not cause much of a reaction in Chico. People had become accustomed to seeing me in my bandages and hardly noticed the change. Since I was allowed to take my mask off for meals, some of my new friends saw my face for the first time. They were all quick to tell me how good I looked.

My mother had not been able to visit me before my release from the hospital. At the time of the accident she had been about to enter the hospital for gall bladder surgery. The surgery had been successful, but it was several weeks before her doctor gave her permission to travel. She had wanted to visit me just before my discharge from the hospital but was discouraged by Dr. Morgan. He apparently told her he did not feel I was ready to see her. I don't think she has ever fully forgiven him. After all, as my mother, she felt she should be with me. I understand my mother's feelings but I also understand why Dr. Morgan asked her to postpone her visit.

As much as I enjoyed my mother's visit, it was also an emotionally exhausting time for me and I am sure for her. As a mother, I know how hard it would have been for me to see one of my beautiful daughters injured and scarred. I know it was painful for Mom to see me that first time. She had always been proud of her beautiful daughters and although I know part of her pride in me was for my accomplishments, it was hard for her to see me looking less than beautiful.

My mother is a wonderful woman. She had been widowed twice at the time of my accident and the example of her courage helped me cope with the loss of my husband. The thing that made the visit difficult was that mother believes in keeping a "stiff upper lip." The afternoon she arrived we were sitting in my room in the Holiday Inn. Her eyes began filling with tears as we talked. "My goodness, I must be allergic to something," she said, daubing at them. "I don't know what is making my eyes water."

My mother has never had an allergy in her life.

On other occasions when I would notice her brushing away tears, she would say, "It must be my contact lenses that are making my eyes water."

"Mom, it's O.K. to cry," I'd say.

But she always denied she was crying. I know she felt that if she broke down and cried, I would too and we might both become overwhelmed by our grief. I think it might have helped us both to have been able to have a good cry together. We did spend many wonderful hours together shopping to fill out my wardrobe and remembering good times our whole family had had together. She also got my hair in shape. My first hair cut had left a little to be desired, and she is an excellent hair stylist so she got it in shape for me. The visit helped us both. I had lost my husband and children. She had lost her son-in-law and three of her grandchildren, and her daughter was badly scarred. We were able to comfort one another and to reassure one another that the future still had much in store for us.

The following week I had a visit from another relative, an aunt of my husband's, Josephine Jaeger. Aunt Jo is a wonderful lady, one of the most independent women I have ever met. A widow and retired school teacher, she travels each year from her home in Minnesota to Phoenix, Arizona, to spend the winter. She had written me almost daily during my stay in the hospital and traveled by bus to Chico to visit me. We met at the Holiday Inn and went out to breakfast together. I later learned she was somewhat shocked at my appearance but she hid it well. I thought I looked quite good but my face *was* still rather red. When Jo arrived and knocked at my door I was in the midst of struggling to put on my Jobst stockings. I know she wanted to help but there was really nothing she could do, so we sat and joked about the problems I would have if a fire broke out and I had to dress quickly. Believe me, in an emergency if I had not been wearing my Jobst garments I would not have stopped to put them on.

After a great breakfast together, we went back to the Holiday Inn to rest. Jo had been up all night on the bus and I still tired easily too. Just getting dressed made me feel ready for a nap. That afternoon we spent several wonderful hours remembering Jo's visits to our home and ours to hers. We remembered the fun the children had had at the park near her home in Mentor and at the family reunion we had attended in 1973 when Scott was eight, Mary five, and Laura two. I come from a small family and I remember how wonderful it was to be part of a large family reunion. There must have been over two hundred Bringgold relations there. The weather that early July day was unseasonably cool but the welcome I received from the many family members I had not met before made it seem warm indeed. I told Jo how fortunate I felt to have married into such a wonderful family and how much I hoped they would continue to count me one of them. They have.

Jo and I shared with one another ways God helps us to cope with the grief of being widowed and she told me how much her memories of the wonderful years she had with her husband, "Doe," have sustained her. Here was still another positive example of a widow who was able to cope with her grief and go on to lead a full and joyful life. I praise the Lord for the examples of strength and courage my mother and Jo set before me.

The presence of the Dixons and visits from Mom and Aunt Jo helped me make the transition from life in the hospital to life in the outside world. The many new friends I made in Chico also helped. Several of the nurses and I had become close friends and we often got together for lunch or dinner. My therapist, O. D. Willhite, and his Suzy also became close friends. The first time they invited me for dinner at their home they asked what I would like most to eat. Would you believe I answered vegetables? Eating out in restaurants, I found it hard to get vegetables other than salads and perhaps canned corn and peas. I don't think I have ever enjoyed a meal more than Suzy's pot roast with five kinds of vegetables.

While in the hospital, Father Sturni had introduced me to Dorothy Wilson, a member of St. John's and a professor at the California State University at Chico. When I was released from the hospital, Dorothy invited me to accompany her to the meetings of a prayer group she attended on Tuesday nights. At that time they were meeting in one another's homes for a pot-luck supper and then going to the church for prayer. I was glad to join her although I had never attended a prayer group meeting before. The fellowship was great. I knew they had been praying for my recovery, and after thanking them for their prayers, I shared my experience on Black

Butte with them. I told them briefly about my talk with the Lord and how he had cared for me since I placed my life in his hands. After the meeting one of the group said to me with great feeling, "The Lord is surely going to use you to share your experience with others to strengthen their faith."

"I hope not," I replied. I was still self-conscious about my experience and unwilling to share my story with anyone who might doubt its truth.

Being a part of the prayer group was one of the most meaningful experiences of my stay in Chico. I had never been with people who were able to be so open with one another, sharing their problems and praying together for God's help. God has said that whenever two or three are gathered together in his name he is in the midst of them. He was in the midst of that group, and my faith was continually strengthened by the answers to prayer we shared with one another.

I attended church at St. John's Episcopal Church regularly while I was in Chico. I think Father Sturni charged his congregation to make me feel especially welcome. They did. At the coffee hour after church I was never left standing alone. Members of the congregation greeted me warmly and made me feel at home. Soon after our release from the hospital, Jane Meirdiercks invited Father Sturni, the Dixons, and me to join her at the country club for lunch, and the five of us enjoyed a lovely afternoon. I was also invited to participate in the bazaar workshops. Seems I couldn't escape being involved in churchwomen's activities even in Chico.

- 8 -

HOME!

Home!

My first trip back was a brief one. Dr. Morgan was hesitant to send me. He was afraid the memories which filled my home would overwhelm me and I would be devastated by my grief. I had not told him about my talk with the Lord, although I had told him the Lord was helping me to handle my grief. Along with many others, he was worried that my seemingly good adjustment to my loss might be a sign I had just repressed my grief and that once it surfaced I would come apart. Finally convinced that I did not intend to become a permanent resident of Chico, he decided the best solution would be to allow me to go home for a four-day weekend.

Bud Hartman, who had been our partner in our Cessna 210, flew up to get me in his large twin-engine Cessna 414. My friend Virginia Neilsen, a southern belle from Alabama, accompanied Bud. Virginia is not comfortable flying in anything smaller than a jetliner.

Her flying to Chico with Bud to join me on the flight home was an act of true friendship.

I'm sure Virginia considered the 414 a small plane, but to me it was like riding in a limousine. It felt good to be back in the air watching the ground fly by below. Many friends have been surprised that I was not afraid to fly in a private plane. I was not and am not afraid of flying in private planes. I feel safer in the air than on the road but I *was* glad the weather was good that afternoon. Flying in cloudy weather does make me nervous. It was the weather, not the size of the plane which caused our accident.

Touching down on the runway at Ventura County Airport in Oxnard, I felt I was home at last. Jim Loebl and Bill Peck met us at the airport. On the way home they took Virginia and me to the Pierpont Inn, my favorite Ventura restaurant, for dinner.

The Pierpont has delicious food, and the dining room looks out over the ocean. On a clear day you can see all the way down the coast to Oxnard, about ten miles away. Loving the ocean as I do, I really appreciated my first chance to dine with an ocean view since I had headed north the day after Thanksgiving.

It felt so good to be back in Ventura. When we drove up to the house, everything looked just as it had the day I left over two months before. In September we had finished an addition to the front of our house. Bruce had been very worried about the addition. Our house, built in 1929 in Spanish style with a red tile roof, was very attractive before we added on, and we were afraid its character might be destroyed by the addition. But if anything, the new wing and the entry patio enclosed by a high wall enhanced its appearance. Only the front lawn looked worse than before the construction of the addition. We had not had time to relandscape the front yard and even the dirt was just as I had last seen it. That spring the Ventura Downtown Lion's Club, of which Bruce had been a member, would landscape it for me, putting in new sprinklers, laying sod, and planting prostrate juniper along the steps to the house; but that February evening it was still dirt.

I turned the key in the lock and entered.

Inside, too, everything was just as I remembered. I went from room to room, soaking in the familiar surroundings. Entering Scott's room, I looked at the new curtains and bedspreads he had chosen, covered with the logos of the professional football teams in bright colors. Walking down the hall, I paused to look at the children's school pictures hanging on the wall and thought how fortunate I had been to have such good-looking kids and how misleadingly angelic Laura, our tiger, looked in her nursery school picture taken the year before. Continuing on to the girls' room, I looked at the bright curtains and bedspreads in Pennsylvania Dutch pattern that they had chosen. I had repainted their chairs and chests to match. Hearts, birds, and flowers adorned the yellow furniture. Not a professional job, to be sure, but not bad for an amateur, and they had been pleased. Their spreads were still on the rollaway beds we had been using temporarily until we could buy them new beds. Before we had completed the addition, the three children had shared the bedroom which was now Scott's. I was glad they had had the fun of moving into their separate rooms before the accident.

Our new family room and the new bedroom into which Bruce and I had moved from the room which was now the girls' were just as I remembered. The addition was beautiful inside as well as out! At least Bruce had lived to see it finished.

It had been a long and emotionally tiring day; but I did have to do one more thing before going to bed. I had to call Dr. Morgan. He had given strict orders to call him once I got home. When he answered, I told him how great it felt to be home.

"Who is with you?" he asked.

"I'm alone."

"I'm not sure I like that!"

"The house isn't haunted, only full of good memories," I assured him. "But if you were in Ventura, I suppose I would let *you* come hold my hand."

He laughed.

"Besides, Bill and Edie LeFevre are just across the street. They'll come the moment I call if I need them."

To bed. You don't know how good it felt to be in my own bed again. It did feel empty without Bruce beside me. I found myself staying on my own side of the bed just as if he were there, but still the loneliness was not as great at home with my memories to sustain me as it had been that first night in the Holiday Inn in Chico.

Saturday I made a closer inspection of the house. Opening the dirty clothes hamper, I found it full, much to my surprise. I know I had told people to leave things as they were, but I had not meant my instructions to be carried out *that* completely. I washed and put away the clothes the kids had worn that last Thanksgiving. Laura and Mary had worn their favorite dresses—Mary's a black calico and Laura's a blue gingham, both old-fashioned dresses. I thought again how lucky I had been to have such a wonderful family. The thankfulness I felt for the joyful years I had shared with Bruce and with my children overcame the grief I felt because they were no longer part of my life. Once again I rejoiced that my children's short lives had been full of joy, not pain and suffering.

I know it is the Lord who filled my heart with thankfulness that day. Without his help I would probably have thought only of my loss, and I would have been overwhelmed by my grief.

Saturday evening was the one part of my visit home I was dreading. I was going to dinner with Bruce's parents, Howard and Irene Bringgold, at the home of his aunt and uncle, Linna and Buford Hogan. Both the Bringgolds and the Hogans lived in the neighboring town of Ojai. When I got in my red Volkswagen convertible to drive to Linna's, I wondered if I would be able to shift gears. I still couldn't really grasp the gear shift knob with my right hand, but I found I was able to cup my palm around the knob and shift with no trouble. When Dr. Morgan heard what I was driving, he said had he known I had a Volkswagen he would have sent me home sooner; shifting was good therapy for my hand. I arrived before Irene and Howard and received a warm welcome from Linna and Buford, although they both obviously were bothered by my mask and, when I removed it for dinner, by my changed appearance. When Irene and Howard arrived, we threw our arms around one another. I knew Bruce's parents had really been devastated by the death of Bruce and the children. We were all afraid to mention their deaths and our conversation centered on my fortunate rescue and the good treatment I had received in Chico. I longed to comfort both Bruce's parents and his aunt and uncle

Above: Diane and Bruce's wedding portrait, July 8, 1961. Below, left: Bruce and Diane at his 20th high school reunion, Sioux Falls, South Dakota, July 1973; right, Bruce, November 1975.

*Laura, Diane, and Mary
Winter 1974*

*Scott and Bruce
1975*

*Scott
June 1975*

*Mary
Ocotober 1975*

*Laura
October 1975*

Ready for takeoff, Summer 1974

Scott serenades Mary, Fall 1974

Mary, Scott, and Laura at Maple Lake, Minnesota, Summer 1975

Laura and Mary, Summer 1974

SCENE OF CRASH WHICH KILLED VENTURANS

...ney Bruce Bringgold and his three children ...y when their rental plane hit the side of ...e mountainside, seen aerially, is a ...f Mount Shasta, near Red-

ding. The plane hit (circled area) in fog at the 4,5... Bringgold's wife, Diane, and two other co... James E. Dixon and his wife, Vir... seriously...

—AP Laserphoto

Funeral services, St. Paul's Episcopal Church, Ventura, California, December, 6, 1975 (Bob Carey photo, Ventura County Star-Free Press)

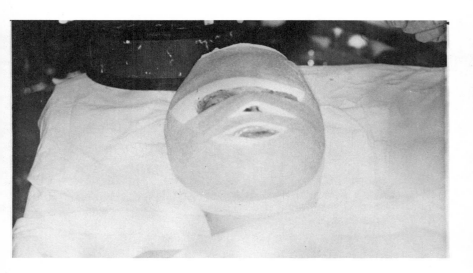

Stages of metamorphosis. Above: Diane, December 2, 1975.
Below, left: six weeks later; right: one year later.
(Photos courtesy of Dr. L. R. Morgan)

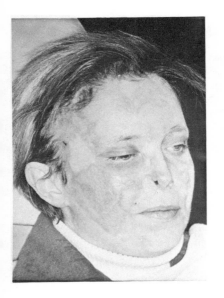

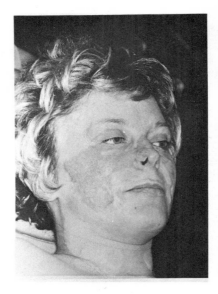

Diane's sister, Jo Ann Melvin, with husband Dan and sons Donald and Dennis

Virginia Dixon, Father Gary Sturni, Diane, and Ann Bachhuber, Chico, California, 1976

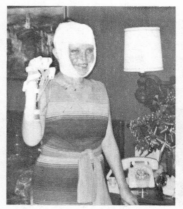

Diane and her "splint"

Diane with Dr. Morgan. She is wearing her Jobst garments for the first time.

Diane, Summer 1978

Scott's 6th-grade class at St. Paul's Episcopal School plants tree in Scott's memory. Below: Diane with Sarah Horowitz, first recipient of "And Furthermore" award, established in Bruce's memory.

and to tell them we should rejoice that Bruce and the
children were with the Lord; but I couldn't find the
right words. Although these four wonderful people
were all Christians they had not found the peace and
comfort that had been given to me. Seeing Bruce's
promising life cut short was too painful, and they were
still asking, "Why, Lord, why?"

The next day was Sunday and I went to church. I had
warned Father Henry I was coming because I knew
when I entered everything would come to an abrupt
stop. Our adult Sunday school class meets at 9:15. I
arrived just before class began and after the children
had gone to their classes. Dr. Morgan had given me
permission to go without my mask so my friends at
church got to see the real me. I received a really warm
welcome, but the best was yet to come. When the
children were released from their classes and came to
join their parents before the service, I was literally
surrounded with children.

"Are you all right, Mrs. Bringgold? Are you sure
you're all right?" they asked. If possible they were even
more worried about me than their parents.

All the children had been deeply touched by the
accident. When we are children we seldom experience
the death of a close friend, much less three close
friends. The children, being touched deeply themselves, really took me to their hearts. Scott's classmates
in St. Paul's day school had planted a tree in his
memory, and after church some of his classmates took
me to see it. It is a beautiful fir tree.

To me one of the most wonderful benefits of being a
Christian is being a part of a church family. Even if I
gained no knowledge or inspiration from the minister's

sermons, I would go to church each Sunday just to remind myself I am part of that wonderful family. The love of my friends young and not so young lifted me up that first Sunday in Ventura and has continued to sustain me ever since.

Monday, it was time to return to Chico. Once again I made the trip in Bud's plane.

Dr. Morgan questioned me thoroughly about my reactions during my visit home.

"Everything was fine," I told him. "I really enjoyed being home."

Apparently he didn't really believe me. Sending me out of the room, he called the office and talked to Jim Loebl and Bill Peck. When he asked them how the weekend *really* went, they must have verified what I had told him. We began to make plans for my return home.

When I left Chico about a week and a half later, it was with mixed feelings. I had made many friends in Chico. I was worried about changing to a new physical therapist who might not push me hard enough, and the wonderful staff at the Holiday Inn had almost made it feel like home. But my regrets were tempered by my joy at returning home and by the knowledge I would be returning frequently to Chico for further treatment.

Home for good. Well, more or less for good. Ventura would once again be my main base at least. Again Bud provided the transportation. The Eulaus brought Sam, our springer spaniel, home. He welcomed me joyfully. Sam is a very rambunctious dog but evidently knew he was a guest and had behaved in exemplary fashion at the Eulaus. For the next several months, whenever I had to be gone all day, he would jump our fence and I would find him in their backyard. He seemed to have decided that whenever there was no one at my house he should be with them. Four cats also welcomed me home so the house was not empty.

I'm not even going to try to include all the wonderful things my friends have done for me which have helped me cope with the loneliness of being suddenly single. This book would never end if I did, but I do want to give a few examples of the love they have shown me.

After I had settled in, I resumed my physical therapy with a therapist at our community hospital, who, by the way, with some encouragement, continued to push me hard as we exercised my hand. I returned to the various organizations in which I had been active, always going to the first meeting without my mask. Later after everyone had had a chance to see that I really did not look like something out of a horror story, I would put the mask back on. Everywhere I went I was surrounded with love. My neighbors—the LeFevres, the Stauffers, and the Cheathams—were a special blessing, not only frequently asking me over for meals but also providing me with a wonderful sense of being watched over.

I began going through my family's belongings, deciding which to give away and which to keep. One of the organizations to which I belonged was about to hold a rummage sale. Most of the clothes I packed and donated to them. Some toys went to our church nursery; a few I kept for visiting children to play with; and some, including Scott's collection of football pennants, were given to their good friends. Memories filled my mind as I went through the children's things and made my decisions. Tears flowed, but they were cleansing tears.

All of Bruce's clothes went to the rummage sale. It was more difficult to decide what to do with some of his personal belongings, especially things he would have passed down to his children. Going through those things—awards, music he had written as a child, a gold coin passed down from his grandfather—I think I realized for the first time that Bruce's line had ended. Even if I were to remarry and have children, they would have no connection to him.

Once again the tears flowed, this time bitter tears. "Why, Lord, why?" I cried to the Lord, asking that he heal my grief and fill me with his peace. Gradually, the tears stopped. I remembered that although Bruce no longer had offspring to pass his family treasures to, his sister Lois did. I determined to give these special family things to her and to her children. The decision made, I was once again filled with the Lord's peace.

Many friends had wanted to help me with this packing up and sorting out process but it had to be done alone. Scott's baseball equipment reminded me of the many afternoons the girls and I had sat in the stands watching his Little League games. Bruce would often join us. How excited we were when Scott's team scored, especially if he happened to hit in the winning run. Looking at the girls' black leotards, tights, and dancing shoes, I could picture both Mary and Laura in their dancing classes. Mary so tight, so afraid she would make a mistake, but usually remembering all the steps. Laura, relaxed, often silly, but having a good time. Sorting out the games, I could visualize all three children seated on the floor playing Hi Ho Cherry-O or the Fat Albert game. Mary and Scott were really good about helping Laura when a game was hard for her. What wonderful memories. Remembering and shedding tears over never-to-be-repeated experiences which had once been part of my daily life was an important part of working through my grief.

The most important way my friends showed their love was to continue to make me feel a welcome part of the group. Many of my friends who are widowed or divorced complain that they always feel like a fifth wheel, that hostesses never seem to know what to do with an extra woman. I have never had that feeling. My friends have made me feel at ease even when the number around the table is uneven.

Shortly after I returned home, Mel and Sylvia Cheatham invited me to accompany them to the Benefactor's Ball. The ball is a gala fund raiser for our community hospital and one of the year's major social events in Ventura. I went shopping for a gown that would conceal my fancy Jobst underwear. I found just what I needed and away I went to the ball. I had been home only about ten days, and many of my friends were not aware of my return. Imagine their surprise. A few did not recognize me at first—more because of their surprise at seeing me, I think, than because of my changed appearance. The ladies all graciously shared their husbands and I danced the night away. In a way that ball was my coming-out party.

Not long after that, I was included in plans being made by a group of our friends for a weekend trip to the Hotel del Coronado on Coronado Island near San Diego. On that trip I discovered there are some benefits to not being able to be in the sun. My burns changed my pigmentation so that with the slightest exposure my skin begins to look like a pinto pony. That weekend as my friends sat around the pool in their bikinis, I joined them in a flowing caftan and a large shady hat. One advantage of a caftan is that no one can see the lumps, bumps, and extra pounds.

I joined a prayer group after my return home. Just as the weekly prayer group meetings in Chico had been a source of strength, so too with these meetings. We really opened our hearts to one another and to God and each week saw answers to our prayers. One member shared her concern over her adult children who had grown away from their belief in God and no longer accepted Christ as Savior. She felt a need to cling to them, to try to lead them back to the Lord, but her efforts were driving them further from her. In the meetings she was able to commit each child to the Lord, to release them. Now her relationship with her children has improved, and one child has again accepted Christ.

Another member received a letter from her daughter after a silence of fourteen years. All those years she had been praying their relationship would be restored, and those prayers were finally answered. One of the most wonderful answers to prayer involved the hospitalization of one of our members for surgery. We not only prayed her surgery would be successful but we also prayed she would have a roommate to whom she could minister. Her roommate was an eighty-year-old woman with a broken neck for whom she had been praying for several weeks although they had never met. She was now able to help this aged woman personally as she continued to pray for her.

We lifted all of our concerns, large and small, before the Lord in prayer. We prayed about the ability to meet deadlines, security in employment, a safe trip, patience with teenage children, and even guidance in decorating decisions. The Bible says God knows even the numbers of hairs on our heads. No problem is too small to lift up before him. I know some Christians feel we should only ask God's help with major problems, but in our group we did not feel we should limit his working in our lives in that way.

Having developed a desire to know God's word and to become involved in Bible study, I had begun reading the Bible in a systematic way while still in the hospital. I found the Lord often provided just the right verse for my comfort. Now I felt a need to study the Bible in greater depth, so I joined a Bible Study Fellowship class. BSF provides an in-depth study of the Bible, taking one book at a time—chapter by chapter and often verse by verse. I gained a new appreciation for the Bible and an increased understanding of the vitality of the Bible as a book of promises and teachings as valid today as two thousand years ago. In BSF I also began to make new friends. It was important for me to begin to reach out.

It was wonderful to find out that not only did my old friends remain true but even disguised in a mask I was able to make new friends.

-9-

THE MASK

I spent ten months of my life as a masked woman. During that period I wore my Jobst mask for at least twenty out of every twenty-four hours. After that we began a gradual decrease, but for over a year and a half I wore it for at least twelve out of every twenty-four hours.

In Chico I had found that people were so accustomed to seeing me in bandages they hardly noticed the change when I began wearing the mask. It was when I returned to Ventura that I had to learn to cope with stares and with questions. Fortunately, the Lord gave me a sense of humor.

My appearance has always been very important to me—too important. Before the accident, if I had been told I would have to wear a mask, I would have said I would never leave the house. I did wear my mask and I did leave my house. Even from the beginning I always felt I looked better without my mask than with it. I never viewed the mask as something to hide behind. I wore it because I knew wearing it would help the healing process and I wanted to look as good as possible. I decided I was not going to hide in my room. People would have to accept me as I was, mask and all. They reacted in many different ways.

Jobst masks had been in use for only about two years when I began appearing in public in mine, but a few people did know what they were for. Those people were very encouraging. They would come up to me and ask if I had been burned, stating that they had a friend or relative who had been burned and had worn a similar mask. Upon learning what had happened to me, they would tell me how much the mask had helped their friend often concluding with, "You can hardly tell he [or she] was burned." I really appreciated those strangers taking the time to tell me how well their friends had recovered. When I still didn't look too great, it was wonderful to know the end result would probably be good.

Occasionally a woman would ask if I had had a face lift, adding that she was thinking of having one and was looking for a good doctor. I would tell her I knew a good doctor but I wouldn't recommend the procedure I had used for my face lift. Although my burns did remove some wrinkles, it is surely not the procedure of choice for wrinkle removal.

Small children were the most open in expressing their curiosity. Often when I was in the supermarket small children shopping with their mothers would point at me and say, "Mother, look at that funny lady in the mask."

If I were a small child, I would have done the same thing. Having been a mother, I knew just how that mother felt; she wanted to disappear. To let her know I was not bothered by the pointing, I would often say something offhand to the child like, "Yes, it is funny, isn't it? You don't always get to see people in masks when it isn't Halloween." If there was more time, I would explain that I had been badly burned and that the mask was a special kind of Band-aid which was going to make everything better. All small children know Band-aids perform miracles.

One day I even did a mother a good turn simply by walking down the street. In a hurry, this young mother was about to lose patience with her child of about three who was dawdling behind her investigating cracks in the sidewalk and looking at the dandelions. Fascinated by the world around him and seeing no need to hurry on, he completely ignored his mother's calls until he saw me. Then you should have seen how fast he ran to catch up with her. He may have thought I was a monster. Another child apparently did think so one day when I was walking to the hospital for therapy. This small boy, about three or four, was playing in his front yard. When he caught sight of me, he began to stare. The closer I got, the bigger his eyes got. When I was even with him, he looked at me and asked, in an awed voice, "Are *you* a monster?"

I assumed what I thought was a monsterlike voice. "Yes, I'm a monster and I'm going to get you."

Apparently my act wasn't very convincing. "You're not a monster," he replied. "Are you a grandma?" "No," I laughed. "I'm just a lady." Then I explained why I was wearing my mask. I did worry about what his grandmother looked like until it occurred to me that his grandmother probably lived far away. All he knew about grandmothers was that they looked different from mommies. I sure did look different.

The only time comments about my mask got to me was when they were made behind my back so I had no chance to reply.

On my way to the hospital I had to walk by Ventura High School. It was like running the gauntlet. The teenagers would never ask me about my mask. After they had walked by they would turn to one another and say, "Did you see that lady in the mask? I'll bet she's really vain. Imagine wearing a mask just to protect your skin," or some equally critical and snide comment. I knew they were uncomfortable and did not know what to say but I *did* wish they would make their comments to my face so I could respond.

Finally one girl did ask. "Why are you wearing that funny thing?"

"I was in an accident and my face was badly burned," I explained. "The doctor is having me wear the mask so my skin will heal more smoothly."

She was really embarassed about the comments she and her friends had been making.

I had already been planning that if I had to wear the mask one month longer, I would go to the principal and ask him for a few minutes during an assembly to explain my mask to the students. I know they would have been supportive had they understood why I was wearing it.

I had been worried that I might be mistaken for a bank robber. I almost was. In Ventura I felt relatively secure going into banks because I thought I was well enough known that I would not frighten the tellers. Generally that held true, but several months after I had stopped wearing my mask I learned about a close call. After one of my talks a gentleman came up to me and introduced himself as manager of a savings and loan company. "I was new there when you returned to Ventura," he said. "I still remember the first time you came into my branch. I thought you were going to hold us up, and I was ready to push the emergency button. But something just made me check. Fortunately, the person at the next desk identified you."

I had two other close calls.

Apparently one day two policemen were driving by just as I was entering the side door of the hospital. Seeing me duck in the door, they became concerned. When I was leaving the hospital after my therapy session, a friend at the desk stopped me. "Boy, did you cause some excitement!" Two policemen came rushing in here about an hour ago, ready to pull their guns. Said they were looking for a masked woman. Thought they'd catch her red handed robbing the hospital. 'Oh,' I told them, 'That's Mrs. Bringgold. She's all right.' After I explained to them you were harmless, they went away."

The last close call was at a Jack-in-the-Box drive-in. I am afraid I almost scared the cashier to death. I always had to take off my mask to eat, but that day my hair was a mess and I didn't want to remove my mask in public. I decided to pick up a hamburger at the drive-up window and eat it at home. I ordered from a microphone several feet from the window and the girl did not see me when I ordered. I drove up to the window, completely forgetting about my mask. When she turned to hand me my order, I remembered. The girl's mouth dropped open. Gasping, she threw her hands in the air. Realizing what was going through her mind I said, "I didn't think I'd hold you up today; I'll wait 'til the end of the month when I'm broke!" We both laughed.

I am really glad I had the experience of wearing a

mask, of looking different. I learned a wonderful lesson. Appearances are not nearly as important as I had thought, I learned. Even running around in my strange mask, I found I was able to make new friends. It *is* who I am that is important, not what I look like. My scars have also helped me to learn that lesson.

I never thought I would be thankful that my face was scarred, but I am. When I was successful at something in the past, I always felt much of that was because I was good-looking—not beautiful perhaps, but attractive. Although everyone always says it is our inner beauty that counts, I really didn't believe it. Well, now I know it's true. I have come to learn that it is *not* how we look that counts as long as we look our best; it is how we feel about ourselves. If we feel good about ourselves, if we let God's love shine through us, that inner beauty will be seen and any scars or irregular features will not be noticed.

I seldom think about the scars on my hands or face. My right hand is badly scarred. The only normal digit is my thumb. I have no fingernails and the last joints of both my ring and little fingers are gone. No one ever notices that my hand is different. I have found people don't always see things as they are; they see what they expect to see. They expect to see a normal hand because I use it normally and don't try self-consciously to hide it. They don't notice the deformity until *I* point it out.

Even my facial scars have not been difficult to adjust to, but then those scars really are not very bad. The first month or two after the bandages were removed, I did sometimes look in the mirror and, falling on my bed (my bed is my favorite place for crying), I would cry and tell the Lord I didn't want to be ugly (I really wasn't), that I wanted to look just like I had before. After getting it out of my system I would thank him for the beautiful lessons I was learning. I would thank him for teaching me I am loved for myself. While I am thankful, I have had the experience of looking less than beautiful, I will admit. I am also thankful for the excellent medical care I have received, for Dr. Morgan's skilled fingers which continue to work to remove my scars and restore my appearance.

Strangely enough, although I have never felt like hiding my hand or covering my face, I have been very self-conscious about the scarring on my legs. I have only a small graft on the lower part of my right leg but I do have a skin graft on my left leg from the ankle almost to the knee. The grafted skin looks great, but where the graft ends there is a raised purple line. I feel fortunate that boots and longer skirts have become popular because they hide that line. Removing it is one of our remaining projects. The donor sites or areas where skin was taken for the grafts on my inner and outer thighs have some areas which have remained raised and red, but I am not really as concerned about them. I am really past the age for miniskirts even if they should become popular again. As a matter of fact, sometimes my donor sites remind me of people who are more than willing to donate funds to a charity or to their church as long as their name is placed on a plaque on the organ or whatever so that everyone will know how generously they have given. My thighs could well afford to donate a split thickness of their skin to the needy areas of my body, but apparently they want me to remember what they gave.

My self-consciousness about my legs just shows I

haven't completely conquered my vanity. Perhaps some-
day I'll even be able to wear shorts without being
self-conscious, but I doubt it. I have hope only because I
have been able to put on a bathing suit and go
swimming even in a public pool. I really have no choice.
Swimming is the only form of exercise I enjoy, and it is
difficult to swim in pants, a long skirt, or boots! That
would look silly. The first time I swam in a motel pool I
was very self-conscious. I still am, but so far no one has
looked at me strangely or said, "Did you see that
woman's legs?" The scars really don't show much under
water. I wouldn't lie on the beach in a bikini and
sunbathe, but thank goodness I'm not supposed to be in
the sun anyway.

- 10 -

CHICO AGAIN

I am writing this chapter in the Holiday Inn in Chico as I recover from surgery. I have returned to Chico for further surgery nine times—at least I think it is nine; I tend to lose count—since I was first discharged from Chico Community Memorial Hospital in January of 1976.

I never thought I would look forward to going back to the hospital, but I do. Returning to Chico Community Memorial Hospital is like returning to the womb. I know I will be cossetted and cared for.

I would probably feel different if each of these visits had not been free from pain. The Lord is still protecting me. I have experienced no postoperative pain from any of the surgeries. I have taken no pain medication. As a matter of fact, Dr. Morgan and I have a deal. I am content with how I look, but Dr. Morgan is a perfectionist and wants to continue making me more beautiful. I have told him he can, just as long as I continue to be free from pain. The first time I come out of the anesthetic and something hurts I'm calling it quits. Now not only do I pray the Lord will protect me from pain, so does Dr. Morgan. There are only three things I dread about my returns to the hospital: the blood test the lab takes when I enter, the injections, and the insertion of the I.V. before surgery. I still have a phobia about needles. They hurt!

I have not returned to the burn unit as a patient, although I always stop by to visit my friends in the unit and in ICU when I check into the hospital. On each of my return visits I have been in a semi-private room on the 400 wing. The nursing staff there is just great, and I have always received wonderful nursing care. The nurses on the floor have more patients to care for than the nurses on the unit so I do not get to visit with them quite as much. But they are always there when I need them, and they, too, have become good friends. Housekeepers are not usually considered part of the patient care team, but even they have been really interested in my recovery. Ginny Garrison, one of the housekeepers, often brings me special treats when the day's hospital menu leaves something to be desired.

When I return to the hospital I always look forward to finding out who my roommate will be. Interestingly, on those visits when I have been tired and needed to be alone and rest, the other bed has remained empty. When I have felt a need for company, the bed has been filled. I have enjoyed all of my roommates, but one very special friend I first met when we shared a room is Pat Wismer. Pat has a wonderful sense of humor. We both had many visitors and our joint hospital stay was rather like one long party. The only problem we had was that

Pat was recovering from abdominal surgery, and laughing hurt. Pat and her husband, Larry, a professor at Chico State, have remained close friends, and I always look forward to getting together with them. Larry is also a great cook, so good food as well as great fellowship is always a hallmark of our reunions.

On one of my first return trips to Chico I met another Pat, Pat Dahlin. Pat is a member of St. John's, and I rather suspect Father Sturni asked her to call on me. I am glad he did. Pat is a wonderful Christian who really reaches out to those in need. I never have to worry about time hanging heavy on my hands. If I am not busy, Pat invites me to her Symphony Guild meetings, takes me with her to her Bible study group, or just invites me to her home for an afternoon. She never waits for me to call her; she always calls me. She and Walt have also opened their home to me.

I have had invitations from many of my friends in Chico to stay with them but because I am usually coming and going so much I prefer to stay at the Holiday Inn, which has become my home away from home. On one visit, I found to my surprise that Chico was in the midst of Pioneer Week, an annual celebration at Chico State, and there was no room at the Inn. The same day I called for reservations, I received a card from Pat inviting me to stay at her home. That time I took her up on it.

The Dahlins are great hosts. Walt, Pat, and their daughter, Per, all lead busy lives and treated me like one of the family. They did not try to rearrange their schedules to accommodate me and I did not feel I had to arrange my schedule around them. When we were able to join together for a meal we did, joyfully, but I never felt my visit was an imposition. The ability to make a guest feel that much at home is a sign of true hospitality.

I always return to the prayer group I attended when I was first released from the hospital. I also attend Sunday services at St. John's on a regular basis when I am in Chico and feel as much a part of that congregation as of the congregation of St. Paul's in Ventura. Father Gary Sturni has been a real blessing in my life. He has been a pastor in the true sense of that word, really caring for me as one of his flock. I like to think that our friendship has blessed him too. Gary, as I now feel free to call him, was only thirty when he first called on me in the hospital the day after the accident. I don't think he had ever been faced with helping someone cope with a tragedy the magnitude of the one I had experienced. Seeing the way the Lord ministered to me in my hour of need confirmed his belief that the Lord's love and grace are sufficient for all our needs. I believe we have each helped one another grow spiritually.

When we first met I felt a little sorry for Gary. He was a handsome bachelor, and I could just see all the mothers in the parish saying, "Oh, you must meet my daughter." Probably they weren't really that obvious about it, but nevertheless I rejoiced for Gary when he met Cindy White. They married in December 1976. Cindy is a beautiful Christian and a real asset to Gary's ministry.

I almost dread the day Dr. Morgan tells me he has completed his work and I no longer have a built-in excuse to visit my friends in Chico every three months.

Chico is five hundred miles north of Ventura. I have traveled from Ventura to Chico and back by private plane, airliner, and automobile. When I drive I usually make the trip in two days. If my destination is four hundred miles away, I can drive and arrive feeling fresh, but an extra hundred miles does me in. There are two major routes north and south through the central valley, Highway 99 and Highway 5. Highway 99 passes through the cities and towns that dot the rich valley floor. Highway 5 skirts the western edge of the valley, avoiding the cities and towns. I enjoy both routes. Traveling 99, I enjoy leaving the highway from time to time and driving through Bakersfield, Madera, or Modesto, stopping for coffee or a sandwich at a downtown restaurant rather than stopping along the highway. Each town has its own character.

Driving north, I have two favorite overnight stops. One is Sacramento, the state capital, where I especially enjoy visiting Old Town and eating in some of the restaurants housed in the old restored buildings. My other favorite resting place is the home of my friends Dick and Judy Wydick in Davis. Judy and I first met at the University of Colorado before I transferred to Stanford. Dick and Bruce had gone to Stanford Law School together. The Wydicks are the parents of two active boys. Visiting in their home reminds me how hectic things sometimes were as the mother of three. Whenever I am feeling particuliarly deprived because I am now childless, I invariably visit a friend just when her children are being their most difficult and demanding. Even the best-behaved children are trying at times, and just keeping up with the schedules of several children often seems impossible. It is as if the Lord is leading me into these situations to show me there are disadvantages as well as advantages in any situation. As much as I enjoyed being a wife and mother, I do remember there were days I longed for peace and quiet.

Traveling 5, I enjoy the contrast between the undeveloped hillsides on the west and the rich farmlands on the eastern side of the highway. Traveling either route, I am always impressed by the beauty of God's creation and by the productivity of the valley. In the spring the hills are green and the valley floor is brown, the fields newly tilled and planted. In the summer and fall the colors reverse. The valley floor becomes green as crops of cotton, alfalfa, and tomatoes grow, while the hills become dry and brown. Easterners often fail to see the beauty of our brown—or as we like to call them, golden—hills but I love the contrast between their pristine beauty and the rich valley floor.

The first time I drove to Chico in my little red Volkswagen, several friends volunteered to accompany me. I am glad I turned them down. The Lord used that first trip to continue to heal my grief through the cleansing power of tears. Our family never traveled long distances by car. We always flew, but the girls and I did make one long car trip together. Bruce and I had purchased property with two small one-room cabins on a lake in northwestern Minnesota, Maple Lake. Bruce's aunt and uncle Bill and Hilda Borchert had a home on the lake. Bill, who had obtained his real estate broker's license at the youthful age of eighty, had sold us the property. We needed a car when we were at the cabins so I drove our old station wagon back to leave there. The girls went with me. Bruce and Scott flew back together and met us at the cabin.

We made the trip the week of Memorial Day the year of the accident. It was a wonderful trip. The girls thoroughly enjoyed seeing the country from the ground for once. We drove east through Nevada and then north into Utah, stopping the first night at Beaver. At breakfast the girls ordered orange juice. "Yuck, this isn't orange juice," Mary said. It was canned, something my California girls had never tasted.

Whenever I drive, I stop every couple of hours. We visted town parks and stopped to read historic markers along the road as we continued through Utah and Idaho. Turning east again, we visited a restored fort in Jamestown, North Dakota. That was a special treat, and the girls each bought an Indian doll. They also bought Scott a knife in a leather scabbard. Both Mary and Laura were very interested in the countryside through which we passed, but I think they were most impressed by the distances. The country seems much smaller when you look down on it from the air than when you travel over it in a car.

My first trip north to Chico brought back many memories of that earlier trip east with the girls. The car and the route were different. The only thing the two trips had in common was that they were both made in an automobile, but nevertheless memories of the girls flooded my mind. Driving along, my eyes would fill with tears and I would turn off the road and let them flow. I still find it difficult to cry unless I am alone, and I'm glad I was alone then. My crying over, I would thank the Lord for my wonderful memories of Mary and Laura. He would once again fill my heart with joy that they had not known pain and suffering, joy that they are now with him. In the Sermon on the Mount, Jesus said, "Blessed are those who mourn for they shall be comforted" (Matt. 5:4, RSV). I was.

- 11 -

BIRTHDAYS AND HOLIDAYS

Holidays—special days we spend with family and friends. I have never spent a holiday alone. Although my husband and children are dead, holidays are still special times to join together with my family and with my friends; but some holidays have gained an added significance in my life since the accident.

To me the two most beautiful days of the year are now Christmas and Easter. The reason is obvious. Christmas is more than Christmas trees and excited children eagerly awaiting Christmas morning to see what Santa Claus has brought. Christmas is the celebration of Christ's birth! Easter is more than Easter eggs, new dresses, and a celebration of spring. Easter is the triumphal celebration of Christ's resurrection! It is because Christ was born and died for our sins—died to redeem us, to restore our relationship with God, and to bring us the promise of everlasting life—that I rejoice. If I believed death was the end, I would not have been able to overcome my grief.

Those two special holidays remind me that death is not the end. It is the beginning of a new and more wonderful life for those who have accepted Christ as Lord and Savior. I rejoice that Bruce, Scott, Mary, and Laura are all experiencing that life now. I do miss my family as I celebrate Christmas and Easter, but I am thankful for all the wonderful holidays we spent together.

Through Christ's death and resurrection we have the promise of everlasting life. But we have more than that. Jesus promised that when we pray in his name our prayers will be heard and answered. By experiencing Christ's presence in our lives, our lives here on earth can be full of joy and peace. The joy and thankfulness I feel as I celebrate Christmas and Easter cannot be adequately expressed.

July 4, 1976 was a very special day for me. I experienced the Lord's healing of my grief in a very real way that day. I spent the Fourth at Bill and Edie LeFevre's vacation home in Dunsmuir, the first time I had returned to Dunsmuir since the accident. Several of Edie's family have cabins together. There is also a large Victorian house on the property where the family gathers for dinner on Saturday evenings and on holidays during the summer. Bruce and I and the children had spent several Fourth of July holidays with Bill and Edie and had become friends with many of the family. Knowing that all the family were worried about me and that many of them had prayed for my recovery, I wanted to be with them on the Fourth to assure them their prayers had been answered and I had recovered fully from the accident. That evening as the children lighted sparklers and ran around the lawn, I could picture Scott, Mary, and Laura in the clothes they had worn the year before joining in on the fun, their faces mirroring their excitement. The Lord filled my heart with joy that they had had that wonderful experience. My heart was not sad. I felt happy and at peace. That moment at least, my grief was truly healed.

I am often asked if the birthdays of Bruce and the children are difficult days for me. They really aren't. Fortunately, I have a terrible memory for dates, and I must admit that now that I am no longer planning birthday parties for them, their birthdays sometimes come and go before I realize the significance of the date. Perhaps the Lord is even able to use our weaknesses as blessings. I do not make a point of visiting the cemetery to place flowers on the graves on birthdays. I visit the graves once or twice a year but not on any special day. I know many people feel nearer to their loved ones when they visit their grave sites, but I don't. As far as I am concerned, my husband and children are not in those graves. Their earthly flesh may have been buried in that place, but they had already gone to be with the Lord. I don't know if they are aware of what is happening on earth or not, but if they are, I am sure it is more important to them to see me happy than to see fresh flowers on their graves.

I know one reason holidays and birthdays have not been difficult days for me is because my friends really lift me up in prayer on those special days, asking that I be protected from grief and that the Lord will turn any grief I do feel into joy. Those prayers are always answered.

I do think there was one holiday on which everyone forgot to pray for me. That day—New Year's Day

1977—was the only day since the accident I have spent an entire day feeling depressed.

I was not alone that day. Bill Peck had invited me and several of our friends to his home to watch the football games. Bruce's sister and her husband, Jerry Zoerb, were also there. Howard, Bruce's father, had died early Christmas morning. Lois and Jerry had come from Canada to arrange and to attend his funeral and to see that Irene, Bruce's mother, was comfortable in the rest home in which she was living.

Howard's death was a blessing. He had felt his life was over when Bruce was killed. He and Irene had never recovered from the death of their son. I am afraid my God-given ability to cope with Bruce's death may even have led Irene to believe I had never truly loved him. Nothing could have been further from the truth. When Howard died, Irene retreated into her own world and repressed her memories of Bruce and Howard. She sometimes told other residents of the home she had never been married. I don't think Howard's death and Irene's mental problems were the reason for my depression that day, but I was grieving for them as well as for my family, and wishing I had been able to comfort them in their loss. I had tried.

We watched the football games together. I don't think anyone else noticed my depression but although I enjoyed being part of that warm group of friends, I was really feeling melancholy. Late in the afternoon everyone else left and I remained. I was sitting next to Bill on the couch and suddenly the tears began to flow. Fortunately, he let me cry on his shoulder. New Year's Day is a day for looking ahead. Maybe it was only then, more than a year after the accident, I really realized

how different my future would be than the future
Bruce and I had planned together. Bill just sat there
and held me as I cried, comforting me with his
presence. Bill's continued friendship has been very
important to me. As I left to go home, I felt better, but I
was still in what I would call a "blue funk."

The day after New Year's Day was a Sunday. Praise
the Lord! Attending church, I once again turned my
thoughts to God and to his love for us as I participated
in the communion service. Once again I was filled with
his peace and with his joy.

New Year's Day 1978 I made sure all my friends were
lifting me up in prayer, and the day passed without
incident. Maybe that New Year's Day would have been
happy without their prayers, but I believe prayer does
make a difference.

- 12 -

THE LORD LEADS GENTLY

Me, stand up in front of a group and share my faith? You've got to be kidding!

One of the reasons I had not completely yielded my life to the Lord before the accident was that I was a little afraid what he might ask me to do. "What if I really give the Lord my life and he asks me to do something I just can't do?" I thought. "What if he asks me to witness?"

I had chaired many groups and I was comfortable presiding over a meeting, but public speaking terrified me. I was hesitant to express my convictions if I thought anyone might disagree with me or ridicule me. Fortunately, the Lord is gentle. I do not believe he ever asks us to do anything without first giving us the desire to do it.

At first, I was very hesitant to tell anyone I had seen the Lord on Black Butte and that he had spoken to me. I was sure anyone I told would think I had been hallucinating. I did tell a few close friends—ministers who were close to me—and members of the prayer groups I joined; but I was able to tell them of my experience only because I thought they would believe me. At least I knew they wouldn't ridicule me.

It wasn't until February 1977, fourteen months after the accident, that I stood before a group to tell my story. During that fourteen months the Lord had continued to work in my life, protecting me from pain and loneliness and healing my grief. I found the peace and the joy I was experiencing as I continued to walk in God's presence almost indescribable. I developed an irresistible desire to share what the Lord had done in my life. When I could no longer keep my mouth shut, the Lord began presenting me with opportunities to share.

The first invitation to share was extended by Bruce's aunt Ruth Borchert. Ruth and her husband, Julius, had visited me at my home, and I had told them of the miraculous way the Lord had reached out to me. Ruth said she would really like me to come to her church and share my story. I blithely agreed, thinking I would probably be sharing with her Sunday school class.

Ruth and Julius attend St. Olaf's Lutheran Church in Garden Grove. Their minister, Erling Wold, has himself received a miraculous healing and I knew his congregation would be open to my testimony.

I was to spend Saturday evening at the Borcherts. Friday I called Ruth and asked her just what I was going to be doing that Sunday. Much to my horror she said, "Oh, Pastor Wold has said you can have ten minutes at each service to give your testimony."

Panic!

I went into my study and prayed the Lord would guide me as I prepared my speech. He directed me to a passage in Matthew. It restored my trust in him and my faith that he would be with me that Sunday. In Matthew 10:19–20 Jesus tells his disciples, "Do not be anxious how you are to speak or what you are to say; for what you are to say will be given to you in that hour; for it is not you who speak, but the Spirit of your Father speaking through you."

As I sat at the typewriter that night preparing the speech, I *was* given the words to say. Each time I speak I claim that same promise.

As I stood before the congregation of St. Olaf's, I knew the Lord was with me. Mentally I was relaxed and at ease. Physically—well, physically it was a different story. My stomach was doing flip-flops. It still does. My head and heart know the Lord will give me the words to say but apparently I haven't convinced my stomach yet.

The members of St. Olaf's received me warmly. Many said their faith had been strengthened by my testimony. It was a great beginning.

The Lord continued to lead me gently along this new path of service. My next opportunity to share was at a coffee for my neighbors, given by Kathleen Parsa, a beautiful Christian who has become my prayer partner. Many of our friends in the neighborhood continued to ask her for reports on my progress. They were hesitant to ask me how I was doing, or, if they did, they did not believe me when I said everything was fine. Kathleen asked if at her coffee I would really tell these concerned friends the reason I had been able to cope so well with my injuries and with the loss of my family. I said O.K., expecting fifteen or, at the most, twenty neighbors to attend. Almost forty came. I know some of my friends did not believe I had really seen the Lord on Black Butte, but many were convinced that my strength and joy were from the Lord. I can understand those who find it difficult to believe the Lord appeared to me. It *is* hard to believe. Before the accident if I had been sitting in an audience and someone had said she had seen the Lord, I would not have believed her either.

My visit to St. Olaf's Lutheran Church in Garden Grove and the coffee at Kathleen's started the ball rolling.

Jim McClain, a reporter for the Ventura County *Star-Free Press*, called and asked for an interview. Jim is an amazing person. He is blind. He lost his sight a few years ago, but he has refused to view his blindness as a handicap. I knew he would write a positive story—that he would not get caught up in the "poor Diane" syndrome. He came to my home, accompanied by a photographer. Because he can't take notes during his interviews, he tapes them. We talked for almost two hours. I thought the story would be fairly brief and wondered how he was going to be able to condense our interview. On Sunday, I opened the paper to the "People" section and gasped. My story covered the entire front page of the section except for one column. They had even used three pictures. As I read the story, I thanked the Lord for guiding Jim as he wrote. There was not one error or misinterpretation in the story. Jim had written with great insight and understanding.

I began to receive invitations to speak at more neighborhood coffees and at meetings of various churchwomen's groups. I loved the opportunities I was given to tell others that we really can trust in the Lord, that he wants to care for us and to make our burdens light. I was sure the interest in my story would soon end, so I wanted to speak wherever I had a chance before the invitations stopped coming.

In May I had my first television and radio interviews. They were in Sioux Falls, South Dakota—of all places. My husband had attended high school in Sioux Falls and his high school friends wanted to do something special in Bruce's memory. Since Bruce had been an outstanding debater at Washington High, they decided to establish an award to be given each year to the outstanding senior forensics student at Washington in memory of Bruce. One of Bruce's friends, Ed Pennock, had designed a statue of a young man debating and had cast it in bronze. Ed's son, Scott, an art major at Sioux Falls College, had helped him with the statue. Ed and his wife, Sherry, were divorced, and Scott had not been close to his father since the divorce. Their relationship was restored as they worked together on the trophy. Just before the work was completed Scott died in a tragic accident. I praise the Lord for using Bruce's death to bring Scott and Ed together before Scott's death. The completed trophy is beautiful.

I was invited to Sioux Falls by our friends to present the trophy at the awards dinner. Lincoln High School has a cable television station operated by the students as a training program. Their instructor, feeling that the story of the trophy and of my experience would make a good interview program, invited Ed Pennock, Al Borgan, and me to be interviewed. The program was carried on the local cable station. While it was a student production, it was well done and it was fun to see myself on TV. Sylvia Henken, president of KS00 Radio in Sioux Falls, was our interviewer. She became so fascinated with the story she invited me to come down to her station to tape a radio interview. I never did hear that interview but I am told it was good.

During my stay in Sioux Falls, I was also invited to speak to a high school class on death and dying. As I discussed my grieving experiences and shared my story with them, I told the students I felt I could not have coped with the loss of my family without the Lord's help. What a blessing to be able to share the Lord with young people.

Much to my surprise I was beginning to enjoy witnessing.

- 13 -

ME, A COVER GIRL!

One June day in the spring of 1977 I returned to my home to find a message left by my cleaning woman. Call Van Varner, it said. I had never heard of him, nor did I recognize the area code of the phone number.

I made the call. Much to my surprise, it was the office of *Guideposts* magazine in New York City. Van Varner is their senior articles editor. He was on his way to Idaho and wanted to know whether, if he came on to California, I could meet with him to discuss doing an article for *Guideposts*. I couldn't imagine anyone coming from New York to interview me, but of course I said yes.

Mr. Varner flew to Los Angeles and rented a car to drive to Ventura. After a lovely dinner at the Pierpont Inn, we returned to my home and began an interview that lasted almost three hours. I had never written a magazine article, so Van said he would be happy to write the article from our interview and send it to me for my corrections before it was published. Working together, a story was written which pleased both of us.

After I returned the story in its final form, I began rushing to the mailbox to get my copies of *Guideposts* as soon as they arrived. I did not know which issue would carry the story.

In September I returned to Chico for more surgery. One weekend after I had been released from the hospital, but while I was still an outpatient, I drove to Paso Robles to speak at the Paso Robles Community Church. When I arrived, my hostess regretfully told me her brother-in-law and his wife had arrived unexpectedly from Nebraska and her guest room was full. She took me to the home of their minister and his wife, Ollie and Donna Demous. Ollie was attending a church convention and Donna was glad to have a houseguest.

Just as I entered the house, the phone rang. It was for me. I didn't even pause to think that no one knew where I was. "This is William Reed. I'm a photographer." The caller introduced himself. "*Guideposts* magazine has asked me to take some pictures of you. Glad I've finally tracked you down. I've already called your home, the Holiday Inn, and the Wirts, the people you had planned to stay with in Paso Robles."

What a detective!

He asked if he could drive up from Santa Barbara the next day to photograph me. We arranged to meet at the Demouses the following morning at 9:00 A.M.

I couldn't understand why a photographer had been assigned to take my picture. Mr. Varner had taken several pictures when he was at my home.

I went into my room to rest. As I was passing the mirror, I looked at my image and thought, "Oh, no! Mr. Reed won't want to take my picture like this." Dr. Morgan had just done some reconstructive surgery on my nose, and I had a white plastic stint protruding from my right nostril, held in by blue stitches. (A stint is a white plastic form that provides support during the healing process and also keeps the nostril open.) I had forgotten all about it. I didn't have Mr. Reed's phone number, so I prayed, "Lord, if you want my picture taken this way it's okay with me—but if you don't, please have Mr. Reed call back." He didn't call back.

When he arrived I told him to feel free to take the pictures from any angle. Perhaps the Lord wanted my picture to appear complete with nose stint so that others who were scarred or had to wear bandages would not be so self-conscious of their appearance. We went to the Paso Robles Inn and used their beautiful garden as a setting. Mr. Reed took roll after roll of photographs. Donna, my hostess, went with us and she and I posed for some pictures together. We took pictures of me walking down a path, sitting on a rock near one of the ponds, standing on the bridge, and talking to Donna over a cup of coffee. I felt like a professional model. I still couldn't figure out why all these pictures were being made. All Bill Reed knew was that he had been asked to take them.

After two wonderful days in Paso Robles, I returned to the Holiday Inn in Chico to find a message waiting for me from Van Varner. Returning his call, I learned that *Guideposts'* editors had decided to feature my story in the February issue. One of the pictures Bill Reed had taken would be used on the cover.

I was really amazed. Me, a cover-girl! Most of those I had seen featured on the cover of *Guideposts* were famous sports or entertainment figures or religious or political leaders. I wasn't anyone special.

Although I assured Bernadette Risi, the art director, that she could use any of the pictures, the one finally chosen was a beautiful picture of me standing on a bridge. My scars and my nose stint didn't even show. Many have written to say that the peace and joy portrayed by that cover have been an inspiration to them.

Because of storms in New York, delivery of that February issue of *Guideposts* was delayed in California. Before my copy had even reached me, I began receiving phone calls from subscribers all across the country who had read my story. I had thought that perhaps a few people might write to me in care of *Guideposts* if my story stuck a responsive chord, but I had never expected people to pick up the phone, ask information for my number, and call long distance. Soon I also began receiving letters. Some were sent to *Guideposts* and forwarded, but most were mailed directly to me, addressed simply to Diane Bringgold, Ventura, California. Since Ventura is a town of 70,000 people, that the letters arrived is a credit to our much maligned postal service. I also believe my receipt of those letters is a sign that if the Lord wishes a letter to reach its destination, it will. I am glad he gave the staff of the Ventura Post Office the desire to find my address and deliver those letters.

The letters fell into three categories. Some wrote to say they had read my story at the end of a difficult day and the story had lifted their spirits and strengthened their faith that the Lord would also help them. Some wrote to share with me the way the Lord was working in their life. Many of these writers or callers said they, too, had seen the Lord when they were in great need of help. Often they reported they had been afraid to tell anyone of their vision and that my being willing to stand up and say I had seen the Lord had encouraged them to share their experience and to believe it.

I think one of Satan's prime weapons is doubt. When the Lord has performed a miracle in our lives, Satan loves to encourage us to doubt the miracle. If the miracle has included a physical manifestation of God's presence, Satan loves to sneak into our minds and say, "You didn't really see Jesus or speak to him. You just imagined it." All too often we soon begin to believe that doubting voice.

The third type of letter I received was from Christians whose friends had just suffered the tragic loss of a husband or child or had sustained a serious injury. They wrote to ask if I would write to these suffering people. I did. I answered each letter I received, and I am still corresponding with some of those who responded to the article.

The publishing of that *Guideposts* story, "A Promise Made, A Promise Kept," was like the tossing of a stone into a pool of water and watching the ripples spread in ever-widening circles. I began to receive more and more invitations to speak. My dentist, John Hughes, and Dr. Morgan's mother, Pat Geren, both asked if they might send copies of my story to PTL Club, 700 Club, and the Praise the Lord show. All three of these programs are religious programs which invite guests to appear to share their stories or their music. The first two programs are broadcast on both commercial and public television network stations. Praise the Lord is aired over the Trinity Broadcasting Network, Channel 40 in Southern California. I told Pat and Dr. Hughes to send the stories in if they wanted to, but I did not really expect to be invited to appear on any of them, much less on all three.

Apparently my two friends were not the only ones to suggest inviting me to appear. When the program director for 700 Club called, she said she had decided she should have me on the show before she got buried under copies of the February issue of *Guideposts*. It was a thrill to appear on each of the programs, but I must admit flying across the continent to Virginia Beach, Virginia, to appear on 700 Club and to Charlotte, North Carolina, to appear on PTL Club did make me feel like a celebrity. Each place I went I met some very special people. Appearing with two such well-known Christian leaders as Pat Robertson and Jim Bakker was a thrill.

Imagine, first a cover-girl and now a TV personality. I still don't believe it. Each opportunity to write, to speak or to be interviewed on TV serves to remind me of my utter dependence on the Lord. I am just a very ordinary person. I know I can witness to his love and to his glory only as he gives me the words to do so. Without God's constant presence in my life, I would probably faint or at least become totally tongue-tied every time I tried to share.

- 14 -

BLESSINGS ALONG THE WAY

Never have I been more aware of the beauty of the world around me than during the last two years. How can anyone look at the beauty and variety which surrounds us and not know that a loving God created the world? The order and the variety of God's creation is simply astounding. Whenever my spirits are low, all I have to do to revive them is to observe the trees, the grass, the ever-changing sky.

Traveling on an airliner one day we flew through a cloud layer. A young girl in the seat across the aisle reminded me strongly of my two girls and I felt very much alone. Suddenly the plane broke through the clouds. Glorious sunshine reminded me that, just as the sun is always present even when we don't see it because of the clouds, the Lord is always there even when we don't feel his presence. Just as the sun's rays try to penetrate the clouds, so God's love tries to break through our barriers to reach us.

As a parent I was deeply grieved when my children

119

died. Painful as it was to lose them, I know it was not as painful as it would have been to be rejected by them, as with so many teenagers and their parents in recent years. But isn't that how many of us treat God? Not only did God know the pain of watching his own son die on the cross for *our* sins, he also knows the pain of rejection. When I think of all the people on this earth—God's creation—who not only reject God and his Son Jesus but even deny God's existence, I weep.

Many parents, after having been rejected by one of their children, would in turn reject that child if he or she later turned to them in need. What great love God has for us. He never rejects us. He welcomes us with open arms whenever we turn to him and accept his Son Jesus as our Lord and Savior.

Not only have I become aware of the suffering we cause God; I have also become more aware of the suffering around me. I try to read the newspaper carefully each night, and if I read the story of a tragic accident in which a young husband or a child has died, I write to the grieving wife or parent. I simply say that I, too, have lost a husband or a child, and, knowing their grief, I am praying the Lord will comfort them. I also offer a sympathetic ear or a shoulder to cry on if they feel it would be helpful to talk to me.

Some of those to whom I have written have not responded. Others have simply written a note thanking me for my concern, but some of these grief-stricken parents and wives have called. We have often become friends, and they have later said sharing their grief with someone who has experienced a similar loss has helped them. In 2 Corinthians 1:3, Paul writes, "Blessed be the God and Father of our Lord Jesus Christ, the Father of all mercies and God of all comfort, who comforts us in all our affliction, so that we may be able to comfort those who are in any affliction, with the comfort with which we ourselves are comforted by God." God has comforted me, and I rejoice when he uses me to comfort others.

I have not had many opportunities to reach out to other burn patients. During one hospital stay I was introduced to a man named Pat Rivers. Pat had been severely burned in a pulp mill explosion. He was about to begin wearing a Jobst mask and was very concerned about how people would respond. He said, "I don't mind running around with my head bandaged. When I am wearing bandages everyone knows I have been injured and they are very understanding and sympathetic. I just don't know what their reactions will be when I show up looking like a bank robber." Pat and I spent more than an hour discussing my experiences as a masked woman. "You know, talking to you really helped," Pat said later. "I figured if you could do it, I could do it." Because reconstruction of Pat's face has been a continuing process, Pat has worn his mask for over two years. I know he'll be glad to get out of it, but he has worn it with good humor.

One of the major changes in my life is that since the accident I have consciously tried to place my life in the Lord's hands and to follow where he leads. I am often asked how I know what the Lord's will is for my life. The Lord directs me in three ways: through the Scriptures, through circumstances, and simply by telling me what I should do.

Often when I am discouraged I ask the Lord to lead me to verses of Scripture that will speak to my need.

One evening in the motel in Chico, I was feeling discouraged. I needed a renewal of strength and of peace in my life. I specifically prayed to the Lord and asked to be directed to verses that would remind me of his promises in those areas. I opened the Bible and was led to Psalm 91:14, "Because he cleaves to me in love, I will deliver him; I will protect him, because he knows my name." The next Scripture I read was Isaiah 26:3, "Thou dost keep him in perfect peace, whose mind is stayed on thee." Then I knew the reason I was bereft of that sense of peace on that particular evening was because my eyes were on myself, not on the Lord. Strengthened and once again encompassed by the Lord's perfect peace, I joyfully thanked him for answering my prayer.

The Lord also directs me through circumstances. I would like to give you three examples. The first involves a lost key. In this instance the Lord was leading me without my being aware of it. One morning I got up and prepared to go to my therapy session at Community Hospital in Ventura. I had arisen too late to walk to the hospital and planned to drive. I got in my car and reached in my purse for my car keys. They weren't there. I went back in the house and began searching for them. They were nowhere to be found, and it was getting later and later. Finally, I remembered a spare key to my old car, which was still sitting in the garage. I found the key and got into the old car, not really knowing whether it would start or not. It did. I arrived at the hospital half an hour later than usual. After the therapy session, as I was crossing the lobby, I met Angela, a friend from my prayer group. Her husband had been brought to the hospital after suffering a heart attack. She had just come down to the lobby.

Angela needed someone to be with her. I was there. If I had not lost my keys, I would have left before she arrived.

When I finally returned home I found my keys lying right in the middle of the kitchen floor. Had they been there earlier, I would certainly have seen them. Attached to a white macrame key chain about five inches long, decorated with red and green beads, they would have been so obvious I could not have overlooked them. What had happened to the keys and how they reappeared on the kitchen floor is still a mystery to me, but I know the Lord used those lost keys to see that I was in the right place at the right time.

The second instance of the Lord leading me through circumstances involved jury duty. Shortly after I had begun speaking to groups and sharing my story, my name was drawn out of the drum and I was called for duty. The panel from which the jury was to be selected was called to the jury box. Addressing the panel, Judge Heaton told us the case would take approximately two weeks. If serving during that period of time was going to present a hardship, we were to tell him. We could be excused from serving on that particular jury and called at a later date. I had four talks scheduled during those two weeks. Silently I debated whether I should ask to be excused or not. Suddenly I thought, "Diane, you keep saying you will let the Lord lead. Let him decide where you should be." I prayed silently, "Lord, you know where you want me. You know if you want me to serve on this jury and you know if you want me to give the talks. I'm willing to do either one. If I'm chosen on this jury, I will take it as a sign from you that you want me to serve, not to speak."

I was chosen to be a member of the jury. At that point I was still nervous about speaking, so I immediately thought, "Great, I don't have to give those talks."

I should learn not to jump to conclusions. After the jury was chosen, Judge Heaton again addressed us. "Ladies and gentlemen," he said, "I want you to know there are certain times you will not be needed in court." As he spoke I listened with amazement. We would not be needed on three of the dates that I was scheduled to speak. I called the program chairman of the fourth group (that talk was scheduled for a Tuesday two weeks later) and told her I would be unable to appear because I was on jury duty. She was not sure what she was going to do for a program and asked that I call her if the situation changed.

The Friday before the Tuesday in question, Judge Heaton again addressed the jury. "Ladies and gentlemen, I hate to make any changes in our schedule, but I will also be unable to meet with you Tuesday morning." I was free to appear at Newcomer's Club.

I don't want to imply that the Lord arranged Judge Heaton's schedule to meet my needs. I believe that, being an all-knowing God, he knew what Judge Heaton's schedule was. He knew I could serve on the jury and keep my commitments to share my story. The only part of the schedule he may have rearranged to suit my needs was that last Tuesday.

The third example I would like to share involves the writing of this book. I had been contacted by Word Books and asked if I would consider writing a book about the way the Lord had used my tragic accident to bring me into a closer relationship with him. I had prayed and asked the Lord's guidance. In a phone call, Floyd Thatcher, vice president and executive editor of Word Books, said he and his wife were going to be in Ventura for his wife's high school reunion and asked if we could get together. Now it is so unlikely that the executive editor of Word Books would be married to a graduate of Ventura High School and would be coming to Ventura just at the time I was trying to reach my decision, I knew it was a sign from the Lord that I was to write the book. When Mr. Thatcher and I met, I told him I would write the book if his company still wished to undertake its publication. We both took a leap of faith. I had never written. Both Mr. Thatcher and I believed the Lord would direct me and give me the skills I needed to write. I have relied on the Lord's guidance as I have written each page.

I have said the third way the Lord directs me is by simply telling me what to do, by speaking to me. Isn't that unusual? I don't think it is. I believe he speaks to all Christians who ask his guidance. Have you ever suddenly thought, "I should call my friend Joan today," called her, and had her answer and say, "How did you know I needed your call?" I believe that thought, that feeling you should call, was God speaking to you—not just a coincidence. When we ask God to direct our lives he directs our thoughts and speaks to us through them.

The examples I have shared may make it sound as if I always follow where I think the Lord is leading. I don't. Sometimes I willfully go my own way. I'm always sorry.

In the fall of 1978 I received a call asking me to serve on the board of I-Da-Ka, the Ventura Lion's Club wives' group of which I have long been a member. I hesitantly said yes, adding that I would need a job that wasn't too demanding as I would often be out of town. (In this organization you are simply elected to serve on the board; the board elects the officers and assigns the chairmanships at the first board meeting.) When I hung up the phone, an inner voice spoke to me and said, "Call back and say no. You won't have time to serve this year." I did not call back.

That same voice continued speaking to me over the next two weeks. I still did not make the call. Pride was entering in. Subconsciously, I felt they certainly wouldn't be able to find someone to replace *me*. At the end of that two weeks, I went to Chico. The first board meeting was held while I was gone. As I was lying in my hospital bed, I was notified that I had been appointed Ways and Means chairman. If there is any job I hate, that is it. I am not a good executive, and I do not like to recruit people to help work on rummage sales, luncheons, and other projects. Instantly I was sorry I had not listened to that persistent voice.

I believe when I was appointed to be Ways and Means chairman, the Lord was speaking to me in that appointment. He was saying, "See, if you don't listen to me, if you go your own way, you'll be sorry." I was! Each time we had a fund-raising event I was reminded that I should have listened.

I do think we need to be careful when we think we hear the Lord speaking to us to be sure what we hear is in accordance with the Scriptures. Sometimes the voice we hear is the voice of our own desire. If that voice or that inner urging is in accordance with God's law and his character as revealed in the Bible, I know it is from God. If it is in conflict with the Scriptures, it is not.

I know that as I try to follow God's leading I will often make mistakes. The lines of communication between us are not perfect. My ears are often closed, but I know that those lines of communication will continue to improve as I continue to keep the Lord at the center of my life and to seek his direction.

December 1, 1975, was the end of a wonderful life. As wonderful as that life was, I wish I had yielded my life to the Lord before our plane crashed into Black Butte. My old life would have been even richer.

December 1, 1975, was the beginning of a new life—a wonderful and exciting life in the Lord.

I claim Psalm 30 as my special Scripture. It truly tells what the Lord has done in my life.

I will extol thee, O Lord, for thou has drawn me up,
    and hast not let my foes rejoice over me.
O Lord my God, I cried to thee for help,
    and thou hast healed me.
O Lord, thou hast brought up my soul from Sheol,
    restored me to life from among those gone down to
    the Pit.

Sing praises to the Lord, O you his saints,
    and give thanks to his holy name.
For his anger is but for a moment,
    and his favor is for a lifetime.
Weeping may tarry for the night,
    but joy comes with the morning.

As for me, I said in my prosperity,
"I shall never be moved."
By thy favor, O Lord,
thou hadst established me as a strong mountain;
thou didst hide thy face,
I was dismayed.

To thee, O Lord, I cried;
and to the Lord I made supplication:
What profit is there in my death,
if I go down to the Pit?
Will the dust praise thee?
Will it tell of thy faithfulness?
Hear, O Lord, and be gracious to me!
O Lord, be thou my helper!"

Thou hast turned for me my mourning into dancing;
thou hast loosed my sackcloth
and girded me with gladness,
that my soul may praise thee and not be silent.
O Lord my God, I will give thanks to thee for ever.

PSALM 30, RSV